EMPLOYEE
SURVEYS THAT
WORK

EMPLOYEE SURVEYS THAT WORK

IMPROVING DESIGN, USE, AND ORGANIZATIONAL —— IMPACT ——

ALEC LEVENSON

SOCIETY FOR HUMAN
RESOURCE MANAGEMENT

BK

Berrett–Koehler Publishers, Inc.
San Francisco
a BK Business book

Berrett-Koehler Publishers, Inc.

235 Montgomery Street, Suite 650

San Francisco, CA 94104-2916

www.bkconnection.com   Fax: (415) 362-2512   Tel: (415) 288-0260

Ordering Information

Quantity sales. Special discounts are available on quantity purchases by corporations, associations, and others. For details, contact the "Special Sales Department" at the Berrett-Koehler address above.

Individual sales. Berrett-Koehler publications are available through most bookstores. They can also be ordered directly from Berrett-Koehler: Tel: (800) 929-2929; Fax: (802) 864-7626; www.bkconnection.com

Orders for college textbook/course adoption use. Please contact Berrett-Koehler: Tel: (800) 929-2929; Fax: (802) 864-7626.

Orders by U.S. trade bookstores and wholesalers. Please contact Ingram Publisher Services, Tel: (800) 509-4887; Fax: (800) 838-1149; E-mail: customer.service@ingrampublisherservices.com; or visit www.ingrampublisherservices.com/Ordering for details about electronic ordering.

Berrett-Koehler and the BK logo are registered trademarks of Berrett-Koehler Publishers, Inc.

Printed in the United States of America

Berrett-Koehler books are printed on long-lasting acid-free paper. When it is available, we choose paper that has been manufactured by environmentally responsible processes. These may include using trees grown in sustainable forests, incorporating recycled paper, minimizing chlorine in bleaching, or recycling the energy produced at the paper mill.

Library of Congress Cataloging-in-Publication Data

Levenson, Alec Robert, 1966-
Employee surveys that work : improving design, use, and organizational impact / Alec Levenson. -- First Edition.
    pages cm
Summary: "Alec Levenson's immensely practical guide shows every organization that uses employee surveys or is considering using them how to make them more effective, valuable, and reliable--and how to make better use of them"-- Provided by publisher.
  ISBN 978-1-62656-119-9 (paperback)
1. Employee attitude surveys. 2. Surveys--Methodology. 3. Organizational change. I. Title.
HF5549.5.A83L48 2014
658.3'140723--dc23
                    2014005294

Full-service book production: Adept Content Solutions; Urbana, IL

Cover Design: Richard Adelson

To Tamara and Eve ~
for putting up with everything

CONTENTS

introduction

A ROADMAP
TO EFFECTIVE
EMPLOYEE SURVEYS

This is a book about improving the practice of designing, conducting, analyzing, and taking action from employee surveys.

Today it is easier than ever to conduct employee surveys, and they are widely accepted for gathering organizational intelligence. If anything, the pendulum may have swung too far: fatigue is often cited against fielding yet another survey. Surveys play a central role anytime large numbers of people are included in a sensing initiative. If the organization is changing, an employee survey can provide critical insights into change effectiveness. Surveys can be an effective tool for understanding the drivers of employee motivation and engagement. They can measure key organizational processes from the perspective of the employees most informed about them—those who implement the processes daily.

Despite the prevalence of employee surveys, a number of common survey practices are less than optimal. There are three general areas where survey practices can be improved: (a) strategy, goals, and objectives; (b) design and delivery; and (c) analysis, interpretation, and action taking from the results. This book addresses each of these areas and offers advice for improvement. Guidance is provided on whom to include in the survey, the issues to focus on, and balancing the tradeoffs involved.

The intended audience for the book includes both people who are responsible for designing and implementing employee surveys and those who use them, including HR leaders and practitioners, organizational development (OD) practitioners, and organizational leaders who oversee or use survey results. To keep the content accessible to as broad an audience as possible, a balance was struck between comprehensiveness and length and between more and less technical topics. This means that sometimes a topic is discussed in brief and, where appropriate, sources for additional information are provided.

Part one addresses common practices around employee survey goals, objectives, and methods that lead to suboptimal administrations. Surveys can be very long and cover too many topics. The target survey population often spans dissimilar business units, functions, roles, geographies, and groups of employees. Surveys often are promoted as measuring "critical" employee attitudes like engagement without a clear business case for how those attitudes impact organizational effectiveness and performance. The answers for these challenges are covered in chapters one through three.

Chapter one addresses survey purpose. Recognize the limitations of surveys. Don't overuse them or use only surveys when other types of assessments might be preferred or complementary, including interviews, focus groups, archival data analysis, direct observation, and so on. Start with defined outcomes that provide maximum support to top organizational priorities. Choose one or two top priorities and focus on them. Be clear about the organizational level best suited for addressing the survey priorities. Addressing multiple levels in the same survey is doable but harder than sticking to one level as the primary focus.

Chapter two focuses on determining the right degree of emphasis on employee engagement. Contrary to common perception about the importance of employee engagement, monitoring and acting to improve employee attitudes is not advisable for most roles as a way to improve business performance. The benefits of improved employee attitudes accrue first and foremost to the employees. Whether the business subsequently benefits depends on the role and context. In certain customer-facing roles, there can be a causal link between employee engagement and business performance. In all other roles the link is tenuous at best and more likely is reversed: employee attitudes improve when business performance is high. Measures of employee engagement are best used as lagging or coincident indicators of business performance, not leading indicators.

How to match the appropriate measurements to the processes, roles, and teams is covered in chapter three. Choose survey questions most appropriate for the primary roles and processes that are the survey focus. The issues that most matter usually are not the same for people in different roles, functions, and geographies; when there are large dissimilarities, it is difficult to effectively address the highest priorities for everyone in a single survey. Even though you can include both individually focused and group-focused measurements, it is very hard to measure well both individual- and group-level issues in the same survey.

Part two addresses survey design and delivery. Despite the proliferation of consulting companies and online software offering tools and guidance, a number of common practices are anything but best in class. Survey questions often are designed without deep knowledge of good survey practices, leading to inaccurate measurements. Opportunities to improve response rates and measurement accuracy are missed. The benefits of matching survey to organizational data are often unrealized. The answers for these challenges are covered in chapters four and five.

Chapter four reviews good survey design practices. Choose survey questions that are clear and to the point and have response codes that maximize ease and accuracy of the responses. Don't reinvent the wheel; there are many sources for survey questions already written, especially validated questions from the research literature. Minimize tinkering with survey question wording by organizational stakeholders; it is more productive to focus their energies on using the data to support organizational processes and drive change. Use multiple questions to increase the accuracy of measurement while minimizing overall survey length to encourage high response rates.

Chapter five addresses the tradeoff between anonymity and insights. Matching survey responses with other data is needed to show a link to business performance. For employees like salespeople with clear performance metrics, the matching is best when it can happen at the individual employee level. Keeping the identity of survey respondents anonymous is the best way to ensure that they will feel comfortable answering all questions honestly. With anonymous survey responses, however, matching with other data can take place only at the group level. Ensuring anonymity or confidentiality is needed to encourage survey respondents to be honest about sensitive issues. Do not ask for extremely detailed demographic information that could be used to reverse engineer privacy controls and reveal people's identities in a supposedly anonymous survey. There is a tradeoff between maximum data matching and complete anonymity: choose the right balance for the survey strategy.

Part three addresses analysis, interpretation, and action taking. The desire to make the survey results easy to understand often leads to overusing simplified indexes that combine too many different issues together. Conclusions are reached using analysis that ignores the power of statistical modeling. Action taking decisions too often are based on external benchmarking and not often enough on internal benchmarking. Surveys are designed and implemented with insufficient upfront stakeholder engagement to ensure appropriate action taking. The answers for these challenges are covered in chapters six through nine.

The tradeoff between simple messages and actionable insights is addressed in chapter six. Simple composite indexes are good at capturing general employee moods, but combining multiple measures into a single index usually yields insights no different than a single question on job satisfaction. For deeper actionable insights that can guide leadership decision making, focus on the components of the index, not the aggregated index score. Employee engagement is best measured by focusing on the specific employee attitude(s) you care most about: intention to turnover, job satisfaction, thriving, commitment, and so on.

Chapter seven covers statistical modeling. Analyzing average responses to a survey question or correlations between questions are the most common ways of engaging with survey data, yet they are rarely actionable on their own. Statistical models of employee attitudes yield the deepest insights into the factors that matter for employee engagement, retention, and so on. The results of complex statistical modeling must be presented in a way that all stakeholders can interpret. Survey vendors' and internal experts' statistical skills are typically underutilized and should be better leveraged for testing statistical models.

The right way to do benchmarking and interpretation of survey results is tackled in chapter eight. Benchmarking employee survey data to other organizations' data is widely practiced but not very informative and virtually never actionable. More actionable insights are available from internal benchmarking when it is an "apples-to-apples" comparison of similar roles and work settings and when it is the same group over time. Before you can conclude that two benchmarking numbers are different, you have to consider both statistical significance and practical significance. If the data do not support a difference that is both statistically and practically significant, then it may be due to random factors and almost never is actionable without other corroborating data or information.

Chapter nine covers reporting and taking action. Closely tie survey reporting back to the purpose and desired outcomes for the survey. This will minimize extraneous analysis. Engage the organization under study as broadly as possible in the feedback process. Tailor reporting as needed by role, function, business unit, and so on. Involve key stakeholders early and often in the data collection and analysis process to ensure the greatest likelihood of effective action taking.

At various points throughout the book, references are made to specific survey constructs—sets of questions that together measure a single concept. Examples of specific survey items that can be used for many of these constructs are available in the Resources section at the end of the book.

The book is laid out in order of how surveys are usually designed, conducted, and analyzed, with survey strategy and design coming first. Each chapter stands alone and can be read separately. However, if you would like to get the full benefit of the content, it is advisable to read all chapters before embarking on your survey effort.

Though the later chapters address analysis, interpretation, and action taking, some of the points covered there have implications for survey strategy and design—especially if your goal is to maximize the usefulness and impact of your employee survey.

part one

SURVEY GOALS, OBJECTIVES, AND METHODS

chapter one

GOALS

DEFINE A CLEAR SURVEY PURPOSE

Conducting an effective employee survey requires a substantial amount of time, energy, and resources. You have to have a clear purpose for the survey, and the questions need to be worded accurately. You should minimize survey length to yield a response rate that is sufficient for scientific accuracy. The results should be presented in a format that maximizes usability, and you need to engage all of the relevant stakeholders in the feedback and action-taking process. These and more principles hold for all surveys regardless of length—even short "pulse" surveys.

Each chapter of this book addresses one or more of these aspects. In this chapter we start with **purpose**.

Recognize the objectives and tradeoffs. A theme that runs through this book is that there are tradeoffs in employee survey design. You can't have a survey that does everything for everyone while being short enough to elicit high response rates, so you have to choose one primary purpose—two at the most—and stay true to the purpose when deciding what to include and exclude. This means selecting the desired outcomes for the survey and the right organizational level or levels on which to focus. It also means recognizing the limitations of surveys.

Surveys are good for gathering information in a focused way from a large group of people. A survey can collect a lot of data quickly and cheaply, but it might increase decision-making time. Stakeholder interviews alone may identify the organizational issues to be addressed. Archival analysis of data in your IT systems may provide a sufficient assessment. Direct observation of people and processes might reveal sufficient information for action taking without further investigation.

Surveys are best used when integrated with other assessment approaches. Interviews and focus groups of key stakeholders are often needed to define the scope of a survey. Archival data analysis and direct observation, if conducted before or during the survey design phase, can provide complementary information to help refine the survey scope. Alternatively, a survey analysis might identify issues requiring additional investigation. Interviews and focus groups can probe complex issues in ways that surveys cannot easily measure. Archival data analysis and direct observation can provide data that validate the initial conclusions of a survey analysis.

Many organizations, especially large ones, conduct enterprise-wide annual or biannual employee surveys. Conducting a survey across employees in different roles doing different things involves tradeoffs. You survey diverse people from different backgrounds who experience different things at work and whose prospects for rewards, development and promotions, influence and authority, and so on are different. You have to decide to focus primarily on individual employee issues (such as motivation, turnover, etc.), business process issues (such as group dynamics, collaboration, cross-functional collaboration, etc.), or both.

For example, administrative assistants, researchers/engineers, salespeople, laborers, truck drivers, and software programmers all have different competencies, roles, and responsibilities. They have unique career paths both internally (within your organization) and externally. Organizational processes—R&D, sales, marketing, logistics/distribution, supply chain, IT, HR, finance, and so on—focus on very different things. If you try to use one set of questions for all employees or organizational processes, you will need to reduce the focus to the most common denominators or run the risk that entire portions of the survey will be irrelevant to the people answering it or to the leaders who have to act on it. The alternative is a survey so long it is a burden to fill out. A better solution is different surveys with different focal points for different departments.

When designing the survey sample, it is important to acknowledge the potential risks of leaving people out. If a group or unit is excluded from a survey for no logical reason and if no reasonable justification is communicated, then people might question the survey purpose and undermine its support. To mitigate this, any survey sample limits should be clearly linked to the survey strategy and communicated to the organization.

The key lies in striking the right balance. An enterprise-wide survey that tries to be all things to all people with the same questions every year is going to have significant gaps. Targeted one-time surveys of specific units, processes, or roles will always get deeper insights into the most critical current issues for those groups. The big, broad approach's greatest benefit comes from focusing everyone in the organization on one topic in a cost-effective manner while not overselling the benefits.

Desired outcomes for the survey. A survey should never be conducted without a goal in mind. Measurement alone is not enough to justify a survey. A survey is just one step in a greater process of some kind of organizational initiative or sensing effort, such as improving morale, setting the stage for a reorganization, improving operational effectiveness, and so on.

There are many potential desired outcomes for an employee survey: improved employee retention or engagement, customer service, quality, work processes, organizational climate, change effectiveness, talent management, and more. The first challenge is selecting the highest priority outcome or set of outcomes. Effectively addressing multiple outcomes in the same survey is possible; however, if they are closely related the survey will be shorter, and both clarity of purpose and ease of responding will be greater.

For example, change may be a high priority. If the organization is about to undergo substantial change or if the goal is to assess organizational agility, then change readiness is an appropriate focus. If the organization is undergoing or recently underwent significant change, then measuring change impact likely is more appropriate. While both change readiness and change impact are aspects of change, rigorous measurement of each requires a significant number of different survey questions. Measuring both well could easily mean a long survey with little room for anything else.

For a second example, understanding employee retention is always useful. Yet retention is not equally important for all settings and roles. For roles with difficult to replace capabilities, the cost of attrition and importance of retention are high, even if turnover might be relatively low. An example of a role like this is general managers with deep organizational and cross-functional knowledge. For roles with capabilities that are easy to replace, where new entrants can quickly get to full productivity, the importance of retention is low, even if turnover is high. A role like this is a call center job for "cold call" marketing of credit cards, where a minimal amount of training is needed, turnover does not affect the productivity of other employees, and employees can get up to full productivity in a relatively short amount of time. In contrast, there are other call center jobs that are highly complex, requiring a wide and deep knowledge base and significant training and experience. In these instances, the role is hard and expensive to replace and desired retention is high.

Thus retention's importance depends on the role's capabilities and turnover's impact on those capabilities and organizational effectiveness. Retention likelihood can be measured using a small number of questions on intention to turnover. Yet measuring intention to turnover is different from understanding what drives people to leave; that requires a full model including factors such as opportunities for development and promotion, pay satisfaction, supervisor support, how supportive and productive coworkers are, and more. So if retention is an important organizational priority, an entire survey easily could be dedicated to measuring the factors behind it.

The more committed leadership is to achieving the survey goal, the better you will be able to focus attention and resources on doing the measurement. However, the survey must be an impartial measurement of the situation and factors impacting the survey goal. A survey should never be crafted to lead to a predetermined outcome.

For example, suppose senior leaders want to increase the productivity of a workforce that is already working long hours and complaining informally about too much work. Someone might suggest a survey highlighting only the positive aspects of working there to show a dedicated and committed workforce ready to take on any challenge, including more work. Such a survey might focus only on readiness to take on new challenges and the opportunities for learning, development, and career advancement. Those measurements are important but tell only one-half of the story. Additional measurements of work-life balance/burnout, intention to turnover, and organizational commitment should also be included for impartial measurement that truly gauges whether people are at the breaking point and cannot handle a greater workload; with these in hand a more accurate assessment could be made of the potential negative impacts of an increased workload.

Designing a survey that impartially measures the survey goal is important for keeping employees engaged in the process and increasing participation. Employees always have some sense of the issues being addressed in a survey: it is impossible to keep the true objective hidden. If a survey is poorly designed to measure a predetermined outcome, the first employees to take the survey will realize this and spread the word among their peers. That will lead to lower response rates and increased mistrust in management for fielding the survey—the exact opposite results you want to accomplish.

Organizational levels to target. Generally speaking there are three different organizational levels: (i) individual employees or roles; (ii) teams, work groups, or functions; and (iii) business units or the entire organization. There are two separate but related organizational level issues for employee surveys: question wording and the level of analysis. Chapter three has a detailed discussion of both issues. Here we address level of analysis specifically related to survey purpose.

The types of questions that can be asked effectively vary across the levels:

- ✓ Issues of retention and motivation often are best addressed at the individual employee or role level.

- ✓ Work processes and work group climate often are best addressed at the team or work group level.

- ✓ Organizational climate often is best addressed at the business unit or entire organization level.

Other question types can apply across levels. For example, change readiness, change effectiveness, and perceived organizational effectiveness can be measured at each level.

Even if an issue can be addressed across levels, its importance across the levels depends on the survey objectives. Though surveys are filled out by individuals, many key insights occur at the function, work group, business unit, and enterprise levels. It is important to clarify the desired level of the organizational outcomes and adjust the survey focus accordingly. For example:

✓ Change readiness can be measured at the individual level. However, organizational change effectiveness occurs at the work group level and higher.

✓ Relationship with supervisor can effectively predict employee engagement and retention at the individual level. At higher levels, it can gauge managerial training and effectiveness.

The ultimate issue is survey length and accuracy. It is important to conduct measurements at the appropriate level that are as accurate as possible. If multiple levels measurement is a high priority, then that should be the survey purpose. If not, then use single-level measurement to minimize survey length.

Summary of Key Points from This Chapter

- ✔ Recognize the limitations of surveys. Don't overuse them. Combine them with other assessment types as appropriate (interviews, focus groups, archival data analysis, direct observation, etc.).

- ✔ Choose desired survey outcomes to maximize support of top organizational priorities. Choose one or two top priorities to focus on.

- ✔ Clarify the highest priority organizational level for the survey priorities. Addressing multiple levels in the same survey is doable; choosing one primary level is more manageable.

chapter two

OBJECTIVES

THE PROS AND CONS OF FOCUSING ON EMPLOYEE ENGAGEMENT

Today there are many survey vendors and consultants who claim a strong link between employee engagement and improved business outcomes. This makes intuitive sense: if our employees aren't engaged, how could they ever work the way we want them to? Don't engaged workers equal productive workers? The answer is sometimes but not always.

Focusing your employee survey on engagement is highly recommended if there is a strong link between engagement and performance. Yet what we can measure on engagement typically is quite different than what we want to know, and that measurement can be linked to organizational performance only in certain settings that are the exception, not the rule. In this chapter we address **whether and how employee engagement measures are actionable**. That knowledge is needed before deciding to include them as core part of a survey.

The not-so-causal link between employee engagement and performance. We know from decades of research that performance leads to job satisfaction. When people are productive, accomplish their objectives, get good feedback on their performance, and are rewarded for being productive, they usually are satisfied with their jobs. So it is accurate to say that job performance causes job satisfaction.

While the counterargument makes intuitive sense—employee engagement causes performance—it does not necessarily hold empirically. Consider this: the easiest way to make most employees happy is to keep their compensation the same and cut their responsibilities in half. Who wouldn't want less pressure for the same rewards? That certainly would make me happy! Yet doing so would completely destroy organizational performance. Thus an increase in employee engagement does not automatically "cause" profit to increase, and neither does it necessarily positively affect organizational performance.

It absolutely is true that employee engagement measures and business results go hand in hand because of the causal link from job performance to job satisfaction. Yet they are statistically related because they are correlated:

the causation usually runs from better business results to engagement, not the other way around. Even when you can show statistically that increased engagement in one year precedes increased business performance in the following year, as Harter, Schmidt, and Hayes (2002) showed using the Gallup data, that does not prove causation.

The reason why increases in employee engagement can appear to statistically precede increases in business performance is because both trend up together at the same time due a virtuous spiral. When performance is going well, engagement tends to improve, which helps support further increases in business performance, which further enhances employee engagement, and so on. The opposite tends to occur when things go poorly: falling business performance causes morale to drop, which hinders improvements in performance, which further hurts morale, and so on.

For these reasons, a test of whether employee engagement precedes business performance can yield a statistically significant result, but the logic of setting up the statistical models to be tested this way cannot be justified across a broad set of organizations, work settings, and roles. It creates a false positive result: the statistics appear to confirm the hypothesis that engagement causes performance, yet they equally well support the conclusion that the relationship goes the other way around.

Consider also this counterexample: when was the last time a business ever had employee engagement scores fall in the year *before* business results deteriorated? If employee engagement was such a strong driver of business performance we would have more documented cases of this than would fill up an encyclopedia. Instead, virtually every time, business results fall first, and that causes morale to fall for two reasons. First, people feel worse because the business is not achieving the goals established by the leaders, which puts everyone in a bad mood. Secondly, decreased sales lead the organization to pull back from doing things to boost employee morale (all the "discretionary" things that are deemed nonessential). So for both of these reasons it can never be automatically assumed that changes in employee engagement necessarily predate or predict changes in business performance, even when there appears to be a lagged statistical relationship.

Does this invalidate the importance of measuring and working on employee engagement? No, but it is important to get the causation right so managers do not put undue emphasis on employee attitudes over business processes. You need to measure both employee attitudes and business processes because, except for unique situations, employees alone do not produce business results simply through their attitudes. The supporting systems and processes have to be aligned and work just as well and may be more important than the employees' attitudes. Don't make the mistake of focusing only on engagement—that would be like putting the cart before the horse—but do make sure they are closely tied together and moving in the same direction.

Where employee engagement does make a difference. There are some select settings where having more engaged employees can lead to increased sales and profitability, virtually all in sales and customer service roles. Employees in direct customer-facing roles can directly affect how customers feel. In these settings, engaged employees can induce customers to spend more or feel better about the customer service they receive, which can increase customer retention. This is the argument very effectively made in *The Employee-Customer-Profit Chain* (Rucci, Kim, and Quinn, 1998), which documented a clear statistical relationship between increases in employee attitudes, increases in customer impressions, and revenue growth.

Yet even in organizations that rely on retail sales and customer service as core parts of their business model, only the employees in direct customer interface roles can sway customers with their own engagement. All the other roles in the organization—from finance to HR to distribution—contribute to organizational performance by doing their jobs, even if they are only "just satisfied" without being "highly engaged." Organizations often can staff back office roles with less interpersonally positive and engaging people without hurting customer satisfaction because they are a step or two removed from the direct customer interface.

Perhaps counterintuitively, increased employee engagement in some customer facing roles can have a negative impact on organizational performance. Consider for example the case of convenience stores that position themselves in the market primarily on the basis of fast service. Sutton and Rafaeli (1988) found that organizational performance can actually degrade when employees are

encouraged to engage more with the customers, especially
when the stores are busy. During busy times, customers
often want fast service more than anything else and do
not want more "meaningful" interaction of chitchat or
even simple greetings that take extra time.

So in addition to survey measures like employee engagement, you need to consider further measures of organizational and operational processes. Incorporating
those other data enable you to paint a complete picture
of how employee attitudes affect operational and finan-
cial metrics. Only once you construct and validate that
larger picture can you know which employee attitudes are
truly causal for organizational performance, versus being
codetermined or even caused by organizational processes. With that information you can determine whether
any employee attitude measures should be managed
for improvement versus used as passive indicators of
employee engagement.

Summary of Key Points from This Chapter

- ✓ Improving employee survey attitude scores is not advisable as a way to improve business performance for most roles. The benefits of improved employee attitudes accrue first and foremost to the employees. Whether the business benefits depends on the role and context.

- ✓ Only in certain customer-facing roles can a causal link be made between employee engagement and business performance. In all other roles the link is tenuous at best and more likely is reversed: employee attitudes improve when business performance is high.

- ✓ Measures of employee engagement are best used as lagging or coincident indicators of business performance, not leading indicators.

chapter three

METHODS

MATCH THE MEASUREMENT TO THE PROCESSES, ROLES, AND TEAMS

If you scan the topics covered in many organizations' annual employee surveys, you will see some common patterns. There are questions on leadership/supervisors, communication and support, training and developmental opportunities, compensation and benefits, teamwork and collaboration, and effectiveness across organizational boundaries (function, department, business unit, etc.). Judging by the common themes, you could easily conclude that there is widespread agreement about what should be covered in any employee survey. An easy conclusion, but a wrong one. This chapter addresses how to **match**

the right measurement to different processes, roles, and teams.

Why this is an important issue to be addressed. A survey's legitimacy depends in part on most questions being applicable to everyone who is surveyed. To make the largest number of questions applicable to the largest number of respondents, a common approach focuses the core of the survey questions on topics that generally hold for all or most employees, even if the topics are not the most critical for any single group of employees. This is not a bad solution, but it does nothing to ensure that the best questions are asked for any particular group. The most important topic areas typically vary across roles, business units, functions, geographies, organizational levels, and level of analysis.

For example, universal measures for most employees include how they feel about their jobs, careers, the people they work with (including supervisors), and the organization. These are like hygiene factors of the employment relationship: if things are going poorly on multiple of these dimensions, then something is going on that is worth addressing, hence the value of fielding employee surveys with these types of questions. Yet these are not the only things that matter, and they often are only of secondary importance. So it is important to not take action based on these types of universal measurements alone. See chapter nine for more details on this point.

The high stakes of an organization-wide survey. The basic issues involved in conducting employee surveys are amplified when the survey is conducted across the entire organization. Because it is conducted universally, the stakes can be very high: if the organization does not "do something" with the information, it will be viewed as a waste of time and failed effort. This point applies to any survey but particularly when it's company wide. This creates a bias toward uniform processes for engaging with the data and pushing all managers to act on their survey results, even if the depth of insights in some cases does not necessarily warrant actions. So is the solution to eliminate company-wide surveys? No, but much can be done to design, implement, and act on them in more meaningful and productive ways.

The general problem is that you can measure a broad set of issues using a company-wide survey or survey that spans a large number of dissimilar roles and processes, but you will be quite limited in how deeply you can probe. The survey in these cases is best used for preliminary identification of potential issues, not for in-depth measurement. For the deepest insights, you have to follow up the preliminary measurements from the broad survey with a more targeted effort that uses interviews or a one-time, more focused survey(s)—more focused in terms of both the questions asked and the people surveyed. Where to look for differences across roles/organizational processes, locations, and levels of aggregation is the focus of the remainder of this chapter.

Differentiating across roles/organizational process and job level. Differences in employee role and job level drive the majority of the variation in the experiences they have at work. Though organizations often have strong corporate cultures (think Apple + innovation, Nordstroms + customer service, or Walmart + low prices), even within organizations with very distinct cultural identities, employees with jobs in different processes and functions have different roles, responsibilities, developmental opportunities, and career paths.

Consider first differences in organizational processes and functions. Different parts of companies have different objectives and core tasks they must accomplish to enable organization effectiveness and success. Each contributes uniquely to the value creation chain—the way people, materials, equipment, and facilities are brought together to create the products and services for the customer. The R&D function specializes in innovation. People in customer-facing roles are best for relating to and being held accountable for the customer experience. Efficiency questions are most relevant for manufacturing and distribution roles. Margin and product mix questions are most relevant for sales, marketing, and go-to-market functions. Human resources professionals must balance the needs of the organization with the needs of the people.

An employee survey can be an extremely effective way of measuring alignment around key organizational processes such as these. Yet the deepest insights are gained when very specific questions are addressed by the people who are closest to the functions and processes responsible for that part of the value creation chain. An employee survey that spans multiple parts of the value creation chain faces an uphill challenge when trying to both derive deep insights and maximize the number of questions that are applicable to as many of the survey participants as possible. Targeted interviews and surveys usually are best for deriving the insights needed to improve organizational processes.

Alternatively, consider how people experience the different parts of the HR system, such as compensation and benefits. Every company has senior executives and much-less-well-paid blue-collar and pink-collar frontline employees (pink collar = office support occupations like administrative assistants, bookkeepers, etc. that traditionally were held predominantly by women). Everyone cares about compensation, yet the role that compensation plays in attraction, retention, and motivation often is quite different for senior executives versus technical/professional/white-collar employees. Blue-collar and pink-collar occupations are so modestly paid, one working parent often cannot comfortably support an entire family on one job, which puts a very large strain on the family's finances. For people in these roles, relatively small differences in compensation (say 10 to 15 percent) may have a big impact on attraction, retention, and motivation.

A senior executive, in contrast, typically can quite easily support a very comfortable lifestyle on one income alone. In addition, senior executive roles carry a huge amount of prestige and power, which are strong motivators for many people in those roles. Thus even though pay satisfaction and pay equity may matter emotionally to senior executives, it is hard to believe that the same relatively modest differences in pay (10 to 15 percent) would have much of a material impact on executive retention and motivation and productivity, in contrast to most blue- and pink-collar employees. Thus the emphasis on pay—its importance relative to other factors, and what should be measured and tested—can be quite different for senior executives versus blue- and pink-collar workers.

For another example, consider managers at different levels in the hierarchy. First-line managers are either promoted from within, are former independent contributors within the organization, or are hired externally. Depending on their prior experience, they may have different perspectives on the parts of the role that are challenging versus easy. In general, managers are more likely to be four-year university graduates, compared to those in nonmanagerial roles. If they supervise white-collar workers, they are more likely to be supervising people from similar educational backgrounds and life experiences. If they supervise blue-collar workers, they are more likely to be supervising people from different educational backgrounds and life experiences. If they are in a call center, they are more likely to have to manage more through direct control and closer oversight. In contrast, managing R&D and innovation processes requires more of a hands-off, manage-through-influence approach. Thus the important factors for managers can vary quite a lot across individuals in the organization, even among first-line supervisors.

For more senior managers, the job is quite different and more uniform. Cross-functional and cross-business unit collaboration is much more important than it is for first-line supervisors. Managing through influence and coaching is more uniformly important for senior leaders as well. At more senior levels, the opportunities for internal promotion diminish substantially; the career choice is mostly between staying with a small chance of being promoted versus leaving to go elsewhere. Countering that, prestige and power may be more important determinants of commitment for more senior roles than for first-line supervisors. For these reasons, one survey addressing both senior and first-line manager issues would have a hard time being both comprehensive and sufficiently short.

Finally, consider tenure. Some roles have low tenure and high turnover. For these roles, issues such as onboarding and the training provided in the first few weeks in the job can be very important determinants of retention and productivity. Integration of new members is a constant issue for teams with high turnover and low tenure roles. In contrast, the issues for low turnover, high tenure roles are quite different. Ongoing development and support for promotion are typically much more important. Institutional memory and knowledge management are usually much better in these roles, but there also is little infusion of new blood and different perspectives, which is a separate challenge. Thus the issues that are the highest survey measurement priority are often different for low versus high turnover roles.

Differentiating across geographic location, especially headquarters versus more remote locations. Geographic location can make a huge difference in the experience employees have in the organization and their opportunities within it. Organizational processes designed at headquarters often are not optimized for efficient and effective application at other locations. Procedures for interacting with central functions such as finance, IT, HR, and so on frequently break down at more remote locations. It is more difficult for remote employees to do their work and be supported in their developmental needs. For processes such as sales and distribution, which take place mostly away from headquarters, procedures usually work well at non-HQ sites but typically better at the larger and more strategically important sites for which they are optimized, leaving the smaller and less important sites to often suffer from benign neglect. Thus what matters to employees—and where to focus supplemental survey and interview efforts—can depend greatly on where they sit.

For example, in companies with large headquarters staff and relatively small remote sites (small sales or service offices or call centers), the opportunities for career progression internally at the company can vary dramatically, with corresponding differential impacts on attraction and retention of key talent. Asking headquarters employees questions about opportunities for promotion internally would be totally appropriate, but asking the same questions of remote employees could be perceived as rubbing salt in a wound: everyone knows that there are no opportunities for promotion locally, so why ask about them when that will only make people upset? Properly understanding the role of internal promotion opportunities in attracting and retaining headquarters employees could be a core element to be measured on the survey.

For remote workers at small sites, a better focus is the aspects of their current job that can bind them to the organization and decrease turnover. Possible measurements include satisfaction with compensation and benefits, the richness of learning opportunities, support from supervisors and teammates, autonomy and decision-making authority, and so on. Of course, all of these are potential factors in attracting and retaining headquarters staff as well; the point of this discussion is to emphasize that there are many factors available for measurement, and not all factors apply equally for both headquarters and remote employees. Depending on the survey scope and context, the best approach for dealing with remote employees can range from emphasizing different parts of the survey in the analysis and reporting to administering an entirely different survey.

For companies with international operations, the issue is even starker. Differences in culture, language, and regulatory environment can make a big difference in the way organizational processes are designed and implemented. External labor market opportunities can vary dramatically across national boundaries; occupational opportunities can vary a lot due to the stage of economic development, the local history of the occupation, and how densely populated the urban areas are. Different cultural norms around working long and hard hours can impact perceptions of overload and work-life balance. Differences in family expectations and social interactions can create differences in the importance of social relationships and socializing with work colleagues, affecting organizational commitment. All of these and more contribute to local differences in the factors that may be most important for employees working across international operations.

For example, regulations make it more costly to fire workers in countries like France and Germany. This can make the role of performance management and account- ability quite different across countries. In low-firing-cost countries, it is easier to use the threat of firing to hold employees accountable, which enables greater em- phasis on buy-and-replace strategies for any role. In high-firing-cost countries, in contrast, a greater em- phasis is needed on internal career opportunities because it is cheaper to demote underperforming employees versus firing them. So a low-firing-cost country employ- ee survey should put greater emphasis on understanding career paths that bridge multiple organizations, while a high-firing-cost country survey should focus more on internal career paths.

Consider further the challenge of conducting an em- ployee survey across countries at different levels of eco- nomic development. In emerging markets like China, India, Brazil, Indonesia, Mexico, and Turkey, employees are much more likely to be the first generation in their family to work in large or multinational companies. Com- pared to employees in developed countries with multiple generations of such experience, emerging markets em- ployees could have quite different expectations for work and careers, necessitating a different emphasis for the survey. Similar to the remote location issues discussed above, the best approach for dealing with developed versus developing economy operations ranges from differential analysis and reporting of a single global survey to implementing different surveys in different geographies.

Differentiating across levels of aggregation: individual- versus group-level processes and focus. Much of HR focuses on individual-level measurements and interventions. Performance management and rewards often focus predominantly on what each person contributes in an effort to promote individual accountability. Development planning, career paths, coaching, and more are usually individually focused. Even the role of leaders, who succeed when their teams succeed, is more often than not addressed through competencies and behaviors that are measured at the individual level.

If talent management and retention in key roles is a priority, then individually focused measurements in an employee survey are entirely appropriate. Constructs (sets of questions that together measure a single concept) such as job satisfaction, commitment, supervisor support, developmental opportunities, work-life balance, and so on can be very important to measure. In this case, the behavioral models that can be tested with such data focus on employee engagement and retention. Yet behavioral models have a much harder time addressing the drivers of organizational performance.

Performance and business success usually occur when groups of employees work together to achieve shared objectives. This means the measurements and feedback should be focused at higher levels of aggregation than individual employees: the team, site (retail stores, call centers, etc.), function, business unit, or geography (city, region, country, etc.). Paying too much attention to individual level measurements creates gaps in understanding regarding group-level issues that are critical for organizational success. If team/group/business unit cohesion and productivity are a priority, then you want to use different constructs than you would for measuring individual-level employee issues. For example, shared understanding about the work objectives and processes for accomplishing them, trust, and cross-functional collaboration are important group dynamics measures. Measuring these can be critical to understanding whether teams/groups are functioning well and to identify how the teams/groups and their leaders can improve group processes and organizational performance.

Of course, it is possible to include both individually focused and group-focused constructs on the same survey. It also is common to report individual-level measurements such as intention to turnover and engagement summarized at the group or unit level. For example, for the survey feedback process a manager will often receive a summary report for all the key issues measured across all employees in his or her group. A survey that addresses both individually and group-focused measurements might have these constructs:

Individually focused constructs

✓ Intention to turnover

✓ Job satisfaction

✓ Thriving

✓ Work-life balance

✓ Supervisor support

✓ Pay satisfaction

Group/unit/organization-focused constructs

✓ Shared understanding

✓ Trust in team members

✓ Organization commitment

✓ IT support

✓ Rewards for team performance

The above are example constructs that could be included in a survey that addresses both individual-level and group-level issues. Yet, even though the total number of questions needed to measure these constructs is not very high (thirty-six; see the Resources section for details), the problem is that these constructs alone usually are not sufficient for thorough measurement. Additional constructs/questions are needed for maximum insights into either the individually focused items, which investigate employee retention and engagement, or the group-focused items, which investigate group dynamics effectiveness.

Summary of Key Points from This Chapter

- ✓ Choose questions most appropriate for the roles and processes that are the survey focus.

- ✓ The issues and questions that matter the most usually are not the same for people in different roles, functions, and geographies. When there are large role, function, and geographic dissimilarities in the critical issues, a single survey cannot easily address all top priorities.

- ✓ Use individually focused and group-focused measurements appropriately. Though you can include both measurement types, thorough coverage of both individual- and group-level issues is difficult.

part two

SURVEY DESIGN AND DELIVERY

chapter four

GOOD SURVEY PRACTICES

DON'T REINVENT THE WHEEL

Despite the many books that have been written on conducting surveys in general and employee surveys in particular, no single book provides all the relevant information in one place. In this chapter I provide a brief review of **good survey practices**. Recommendations on sources for further information are provided for anyone seeking more details.

Ask questions the right way. While surveys are most commonly associated with data collection, I prefer to think of them as one-way conversations: the survey designer has information he or she wants to collect from the respondent and has to anticipate the responses ahead of time, structuring the questions to ensure as complete a conversation as possible. The problem with one-way conversations is the person asking the questions does not have the luxury of asking follow-up questions and does not observe whether the other person understands the questions. This means that the wording for the questions has to be chosen carefully.

Bradburn, Sudman, and Wansink (2004) provide a comprehensive treatment of the issues involved in choosing survey question wording. This includes asking threatening versus nonthreatening questions about behavior and using questions that measure knowledge, evaluate performance, and collect psychographic (activities, interests, and opinions) and demographic information. All questions must be clearly worded to avoid confusion. Double-barreled questions that address multiple topics should always be reworded or divided into separate, more simple questions. For the reader looking for a basic treatment of the issues involved in choosing different ways of wording questions, their book is a great resource. Fink (2013) is another good reference for survey question wording.

Open-ended questions. The question design process includes whether to use open-ended versus closed-ended questions. As Church and Waclawski (2001) point out, there is a tradeoff:

✓ Open-ended questions allow people to
respond from their own perspective,

without being forced to use the response options provided by the survey. They allow people to let off steam and provide insights into key organizational issues. They also are more time consuming to fill out and difficult to code. However, analyzing open-ended questions is easier today than in the past with help from advanced software packages and specialized survey consulting companies.

✓ Closed-ended questions are easy to answer quickly, and provide clear data that can be used to compare responses across people. However, they compel people to provide an opinion even if they don't have one.

The end result is that most employee surveys have few to no open-ended questions. However, a small number of open-ended questions can effectively complement closed-ended questions while diverting minimal time from the rest of the survey.

Make appropriate use of short "pulse" surveys. There is an emerging practice of using very short surveys as part of efforts to take the "pulse" of the organization. Pulse surveys are worth noting because of their versatility. They can play an important role by addressing specific issues that are more relevant or unique for particular groups, and thus effectively complement a larger survey that encompasses dissimilar groups.

Pulse surveys also can be used with much greater frequency, depending on the issues addressed and people's tolerance to be surveyed often. That in turn depends on how valuable they perceive the effort to be. If the survey is designed, marketed, and executed to create insights that are actionable, there could be less resistance to doing a series of pulse surveys over a period of time than to doing a single administration of a companywide annual survey.

Pulse surveys can be used to monitor a change implementation or the trend in employees' feelings on an issue. Pulse surveys can include one or more open-ended items. Despite the difficulties posed by coding, open-ended items can be effective when used well in short pulse surveys.

Choose the right question response codes. How to code responses for closed-ended questions is another part of question design. There are many choices for coding closed-ended questions, including the following (from Church and Waclawski, 2001):

- ✓ Agreement (strongly disagree . . . strongly agree)
- ✓ Quality (very poor . . . very good)
- ✓ Frequency (never . . . always)
- ✓ Extent (to no extent . . . to a very great extent)
- ✓ Effectiveness (very ineffective . . . very effective)

Having a variety of questions with different response codes slows down how long it takes to fill out a survey, but it also has the benefit of increasing response accuracy: when people have to stop and think harder about their response to a question, it breaks the monotony of the survey and decreases the chance that they will quickly run through the survey choosing responses that are all the same (for example, choosing all "strongly agree" or all "disagree"). This is one reason why researchers like to include some questions where "agree" implies negative feelings, such as intention to turnover, interspersed among the rest of the survey items.

Some leaders do not like to provide the option of a "neutral" or "neither" choice because they want people to commit to a positive or negative response, making a clear statement. Yet providing a neutral response is well established as a best practice in the research literature, and excluding this option makes it harder to fill out the survey. Thus it is important to choose either a five- or seven-point Likert scale when designing closed-ended questions so that "neutral" or "neither" is the middle choice.

Where to look for help with writing accurate survey questions. For those looking to create a new employee survey, the good news is that there are many questions available in the public domain, so relatively few questions need to be created entirely from scratch. Published resources include Bradburn, Sudman, and Wansink (2004); Fields (2002); Kador and Armstrong (2010); Church and Waclawski (1998); and McConnell (2003). In addition, there are numerous survey consulting companies that offer a variety of support, such as providing standard questions they commonly use and writing customized questions. The bad news is that even though many of these practitioners have formal training in survey methods, there is no single way to approach the writing of survey questions, and the approaches taken can differ substantially in the choices made.

Survey research companies often claim their surveys are proprietary. Yet there is virtually no such thing as truly proprietary intellectual property when it comes to writing survey items. After decades of published research on topics of employee motivation and engagement in social science academically oriented journals, there is very little that has not been documented in the scientific literature and thus is not in the public domain. For virtually any measure of motivation and engagement that you might want to consider, there is a version that almost certainly already exists in the public domain. Fields (2002) is the definitive reference.

Aside from not reinventing the wheel, another reason to use questions from the research literature is they typically have a long history of testing and validation; we are usually confident about what they mean and what they are related to because of the extensive vetting that takes place to publish in scientifically credible social science journals. If you write questions yourself or rely on a consultant's services, attention should be paid to question reliability and validity.

Reliability means that people in comparable situations will answer questions in similar ways. Validity means that the answers provided to a question accurately represent what is intended to be measured. For example, asking "when" did something occur in an open-ended question could produce answers such as "May 1," "in May," "May 1, 1990," "in the spring," "last year," and so on. A more reliable wording would be "on which date (month and year)" did it occur. Asking questions that address only one topic (are not double barreled) is also an issue of reliability.

Selecting the right response code for a question is an important part of both reliability and validity. For example, if you ask "how useful was the _____ training course in helping you do your job," an appropriate response scale would be "extremely useful/useful/somewhat useful/ not useful." An inappropriate response scale would be "strongly disagree/disagree/neither agree or disagree/ agree/strongly agree." Validity is increased by providing enough response choices so that most respondents can select a choice that is consistent with their views; providing only two choices (example: good versus not good) should produce less valid responses than providing five choices (excellent/very good/good/fair/poor). Validity is also increased by including multiple questions designed to measure the same thing using different forms and combining them together in a scale.

For further details on survey question reliability and validity see Fowler (2009).

Hold the line on survey tinkering. One challenge of using measures that come both from the research literature and from consulting companies' databases is resisting wording tinkering. Typically there are one or more key

stakeholders who want to get involved in writing or edit-
ing the survey items—the larger the population to be surveyed, the greater the number of potential stakeholders
who might want to get involved. Their inclination comes
partly from wanting to engage in the process to ensure the
best outcomes. This can be helpful because they usually
are well informed on engaging with the organization and
the challenges of getting people to pay attention to and
believe the survey results.

Yet these same stakeholders usually operate from a position of being less informed about survey methodology.
They may want to influence the results in a specific way,
whether consciously or not, which can promote tinkering
with survey wording. It is the responsibility of the survey
designers and implementers to explain to the stakeholders the importance of maintaining the fidelity of survey
wording, including communicating the rationale behind
the use of the survey items. Scientific measurements from
the research literature typically have a long track record
with ample evidence of what they are linked to empirically. For measurements from consulting companies' databases, the potential value comes from benchmarking
against other organizations in the database (though a big
caveat about this benefit is discussed in chapter eight).

Allowing benchmarking over time is a big argument
for maintaining question wording consistency. The good
news is that once a set of survey items has been used
more than once and key stakeholders buy into their
value, those same stakeholders can be very strong advo-
cates for maintaining wording so that apples-to-apples
comparisons can be done over time. Yet that strength

can also be a weakness: because any employee survey makes compromises in the questions asked by leaving out entire areas of inquiry, a survey that changes over time has a better chance of addressing a larger set of relevant issues. Thus the survey designers and implementers should communicate to the organization the importance of refreshing the survey on a regular basis to reflect as broad of a set of issues as possible.

Use multiple questions for increased accuracy. Survey practitioners who are trained in research methods use multiple questions on the same topic to create a scale representing a particular construct. Doing so increases the validity and accuracy of the construct measurement; see, for example, Fields (2002) and DeVellis (2012). Extensive research has demonstrated that individual survey items can inaccurately measure a concept due to the one-way conversation problem: though you might think a question has only one interpretation, you typically need multiple questions to ensure that both you and the survey respondents agree on what is being asked and answered.

For example, considering the following questions commonly used to measure the construct intention to turnover:

- ✓ I plan to look outside my company/firm for a new job within the next year.
- ✓ I often think about quitting my present job.
- ✓ It is likely that I will quit my job in the next twelve months.

Any one of these questions on its own measures an aspect of turnover intentions. Yet each aspect is distinct, measuring intention to look for a new job, thinking about quitting, and an assessment of the probability of leaving. Research has shown that asking more than one question leads to better and more accurate measurement of turnover intentions than relying on only one of the items. The importance of using multiple items has been shown repeatedly for the vast majority of established survey constructs. Academic researchers always use multiple items for each construct they want to measure. Practitioners and survey consultants with research training tend to do so as well.

Yet there is pushback to using validated survey constructs, which usually comes from all corners of the organization, because of the multiple questions needed to measure each construct. The complaints are separate but related: (a) "Why do we need so many questions that ask that same thing?" and (b) "The survey is too long!" We turn to next to the issue of survey length.

Minimize survey length for greater response rates. Concerns about the length of an employee survey are related to both the total number of questions asked and the number of questions used for each unique construct or measurement. At first glance, survey length might seem to be a relatively minor issue, yet time and again it resurfaces as a potential problem for response rates, overusing the time of the respondents and undermining buy-in that the entire survey effort was worthwhile. The challenge lies in the following two competing principles:

✓ Shorter surveys are easier to fill out and have higher response rates, so the data is more representative and accurate. They are met with less pushback from organizational stakeholders and respondents. Shorter surveys typically have greater completion rates (fewer partial survey responses) and levels of participation (fewer missing surveys).

✓ Longer surveys provide more extensive insights, increasing the likelihood you will ask the right questions.

This tradeoff typically gets played out at the level of the constructs used to measure each unique concept. As explained in the previous section on question accuracy, devoting a larger number of survey questions to a particular issue or construct increases accuracy of the measurement.

Trading off accuracy, breadth, and brevity. Yet construct accuracy is only one criterion; measuring enough constructs (survey breadth) is just as important. When you add into the mix the importance of keeping the survey as short as possible (survey brevity), it is clear that you can't satisfy all three criteria— accuracy, breadth, and brevity—at the same time. Consequently, organizations constantly have to make choices about what to measure and how to measure it.

There are examples of long employee surveys that receive high response rates. I have even successfully fielded a few of them myself. Longer surveys can have 100 or

more separate questions. I have come across some he-
roic efforts that have as many as 150 questions or even
more, yet those are the exceptions that prove the general rule: going much beyond 100 questions in a survey
is not advisable unless there is a compelling reason to do
so, including clear alignment among all stakeholders on
the survey's importance, goals, and actions to be taken
based on it. If anything, the trend in survey length is in
the other direction. My colleagues and I at the Center
for Effective Organizations have conducted employee
surveys for over three decades. In the past it was easier
to field surveys with 100 or more questions without getting major pushback. Today everyone seems busier, has
greater difficulty making time for a survey, and is much
more likely to suffer from survey fatigue. A 60- or even 30-
item survey can seem too long today if the compelling
case has not been made.

Yet what matters most is how long it takes to fill out
the survey, not the actual number of questions. Survey
length should always be measured in terms of the elapsed
time needed to complete it. Piloting the content is recommended so that an accurate assessment of how long
it takes to complete the survey can be communicated up
front to the participants. A small number of difficult questions can take a long time to fill out. A large number of
easy-to-answer questions can go by very quickly. For surveys with many easy-to-answer questions, perceptions of
survey length can be managed through communication
and smart formatting (for example, putting more questions on a page to minimize the number of pages, and

communicating up front that the survey will take no longer than x number of minutes to complete).

For shorter surveys, the tradeoff then is between breadth and accuracy. Based on common practice, it seems like accuracy almost always loses out: many employee surveys, particularly annual companywide surveys, opt for asking only one question per construct in place of the multiple questions favored by researchers. Faced with a choice of skipping some key focus areas altogether versus using only one question, the choice seems obvious to many: use only one question. Yet it is more appropriate to use only one survey item in some situations than in others.

For example, even academic researchers use only a single item to measure job satisfaction ("Overall, I am satisfied with my job at _____"). In other cases, you have to look at the potential questions to be included in a construct and make a judgment call regarding whether the questions can be narrowed down without losing too much accuracy. For example, consider intention to turnover:

- ✓ I plan to look outside my company/firm for a new job within the next year.
- ✓ I often think about quitting my present job.
- ✓ It is likely that I will quit my job in the next 12 months.

Even though each question measures something distinct, if you elected to ask only the last question ("It is likely that I will quit my job in the next 12 months"), you will have a fairly accurate measure of whether someone is likely to leave, especially people who are close to walking out the door. You would miss important nuances, such as people who are not ready to walk out the door though they are unhappy enough to consider the idea ("I often think about quitting" or "I plan to look ..."), but if you want a short and to-the-point measure of turnover risk, the "likely to quit" question is good enough.

For a counter example, consider supervisor support:

- ✓ My supervisor is willing to help me when I need a special favor.

- ✓ My supervisor would forgive an honest mistake on my part.

- ✓ My supervisor really cares about my well-being.

- ✓ My supervisor fails to appreciate any extra effort from me (*reverse coded*).

No one of these questions captures an overall measure of supervisor support in the same way that the single question about turnover intentions does. If you want to ask about supervisor support and use only one or two questions, you may be better off using different questions altogether; the specific wording used should reflect the key issues in the supervisor–supervisee relationship in that context.

Or consider another counterexample, organizational commitment (substituting the name of the company or organization in the blanks):

✓ I do not feel like "part of the family" at _____.

✓ I do not feel "emotionally attached" to _____.

✓ _____ has a great deal of personal meaning for me.

✓ I feel a strong sense of belonging to _____.

The notion of organizational commitment that has been developed and widely used in the research literature requires using at least three if not all four of the above questions; any less and the measurement accuracy would be so low that it would be better to exclude measuring commitment or to come up with a different way of measuring something similar.

The bottom line when it comes to minimizing survey and construct length is that you have to use the best combination of science, logic, and testing to decide which questions to include. If you use existing, well-established constructs from the research literature (Fields, 2002) and want shorter versions, it would be best to pilot test the pared down versions: find a group of employees who are willing to participate, and administer a short survey containing both the original questions that make up the construct from the research literature plus the alternative smaller number of questions you chose to stand in for them. You can then statistically evaluate how well your smaller number of questions measure something similar to the established constructs.

Summary of Key Points from This Chapter

- ✓ Choose survey questions that are clear, to the point, and have response codes that maximize ease and accuracy of the responses.

- ✓ Don't reinvent the wheel if you don't have to: there are many sources for survey questions already written, especially validated questions from the research literature.

- ✓ Minimize survey question wording tinkering by key stakeholders. It is more productive to focus their energies on using the data to support organizational processes and drive change.

- ✓ Use multiple questions to increase the accuracy of measurement, while minimizing overall survey length to encourage high response rates.

chapter five

ANONYMITY VS. INSIGHTS

CONFIDENTIALITY AND ORGANIZATIONAL DATA MATCHING

Today the overwhelming majority of employee surveys are conducted online. This provides digitally coded data that enable easy matching of individual survey responses to performance and other organizational data. Data matching can provide deep insights into the link between employee attitudes and organizational outcomes that matter, enabling causal analysis.

Yet data matching often requires knowing the identity of each person who completes the survey, raising substantial issues about confidentiality and response bias. Confidentiality is important: without it survey respondents usually won't respond accurately to more sensitive questions. The validity of the data collected from most employee survey questions requires maintaining confidentiality.

In this chapter we address the **tradeoffs between maintaining complete anonymity versus confidentiality** and the **value of linking survey data to other data** to conduct impact analysis when the data are confidential but not anonymous.

Preserving trust in confidentiality. The identity of the people or organization collecting the data can make a big difference in the trust employees have in how their information will be used. It is hard for employees to trust the confidentiality of survey data collected by people working directly for their employer. The people running the survey can promise to keep the responses confidential, but if they also are employees working for the same organization, many survey respondents will not trust those promises, fearing their responses might be used against them. In a world where it continues to become easier to conduct surveys in house as the technology improves and costs fall, this is an important consideration for the survey design process.

Today, most large-scale employee surveys are conducted by specialized survey vendors or large consulting companies in large part because they can provide design expertise and electronic platforms that most companies do not have internally. Employees also trust that a third party won't share information inappropriately with their employer. The aspects of the third party relationship that support trust in confidentiality include a reputation for independence and explicit rules on how the results are reported back to the organization. Reporting rules typically stipulate that there must be a minimum number of responses in a unit (team, work group, location, role, etc.) before data will be reported back for that level of disaggregation. This helps ensure sufficient people per reporting unit so that it would be difficult for managers of that unit to know who provided specific responses.

Yet despite those precautions, there is a tension between the increased ease of customized reporting and preserving confidentiality. Advances in technology and the growth of the survey vendor industry have made it ever cheaper for organizations to purchase reports that are individualized for each manager in the organization. Organizations often measure aspects of the work climate, such as relationship with supervisor/management and employee engagement, and hold managers accountable for low scores in an effort to improve employee morale and productivity. This can lead managers to act inappropriately, searching for the employees in their work group who gave low scores and confronting them directly. The smaller the work group, the greater the temptation for inappropriate behavior like this. The leadership and the people driving the survey process have to include managerial training and follow-up to ensure that the results are acted on appropriately and that there is a mechanism in place for reporting abuse and subsequent punitive measures toward egregious managers.

Matching survey responses with other data for each employee. Matching survey responses with data from other sources can be beneficial for two practical reasons: accuracy and brevity. Some data the respondent either does not fully know or can't be trusted to report accurately. Supervisor ratings are an example of data the respondent is aware of but may not have access to report reliably. Performance data is an example of data that the respondent might know yet report inaccurately. For both of these types of data, matching from sources external to the survey may be the only reliable way to include them in the analysis.

Other more innocuous data can be collected accurately on the survey yet can take up a large number of questions, increasing the survey length. Examples include demographic information, role or job title, business unit, function, geographic location, participation in specific HR programs, and so on. Matching data such as these from external sources can help keep the survey length manageable, supporting higher response rates and data quality.

If you want to do accurate matching, you must know who the person is via their name or a unique identifier such as employee ID number—something that can be used for accurate matching of data from multiple sources. Both ethics and legal rules typically mandate that you let people know that their responses will be identified at the individual level, even if you don't have to ask them to self-identify on the survey. Self-identification is not always required because you can use less obtrusive ways of linking their identity to their responses through the way they access the survey.

Individualized e-mail survey invitations with a unique online hyperlink for each person is one way to avoid self-identification in the survey. This approach embeds a unique personalized code in the hyperlink and is the most subtle way of achieving individual survey identification. A less subtle approach uses a unique login code someone must enter in order to take the survey. An even more direct approach is to have the respondents enter their name or e-mail address directly into the survey. Yet even if a name or e-mail addressed is a required field for the survey to be completed, there could be typos or they could purposefully enter the wrong name or e-mail to subvert identification.

Matching survey responses with other data at the group level. Because of employee concerns about confidentiality, you often can't justify matching individual-level employee survey responses to other sources of data. The alternative is to match based on group characteristics such as job title, tenure, and demographics. This requires creating mean values of the matching variables for each group and treating the group as the unit of analysis. The tradeoff is preserved confidentiality and the ability to conduct analysis at a somewhat disaggregated level at the cost of losing the ability to estimate behavioral relationships at the individual employee level. To enhance the insights from the analysis, the more disaggregated (smaller) the groups used for matching, the better. See chapter seven for a detailed discussion of the power of estimating behavioral models with your employee survey data.

There is a limit to the demographic information detail that you can collect in an anonymous survey. Detailed demographic information on location, department, function, job title, job level, and so on coupled with detailed data on age, gender, race, and so on can be used to "reverse engineer" anonymity for almost anyone. With enough information you can figure out who the individuals are who responded to an anonymous survey. You have to consider that risk when deciding how much demographic information to collect: if it is too detailed, respondents will worry that their responses will not be anonymous, leading to lower response rates, unanswered questions, or biased answers.

This is especially true if you collect very detailed job title information and create the response categories so that the survey respondents are choosing titles that have very few people in the role. For example, consider the title Senior Vice President. In some organizations there are very few SVPs, so the act of asking people to identify themselves as SVP could cause them to suspect that their responses will not be used in a confidential manner. To avoid that problem a more general job title category could be provided, such as "Vice President or higher (including SVP)."

Even if you strike the right balance with the level of demographic detail to preserve employee trust in confidentiality, some reverse engineering will always be possible. This is especially true when survey respondents can be linked to smaller locations or business units. The first point to note is that it is unethical to do this type of reverse engineering if you have promised confidentiality. Even if you have not promised confidentiality, employee concerns about their responses being used against them should be respected to maintain the integrity of the data collection process. This should ensure accurate responses and willingness to participate in both the current and future surveys. You need strong controls among the people who administer the survey and those who have access to the raw data to ensure that no reverse engineering is done. Once trust in anonymity is lost, it can take years to rebuild and may never be fully recovered.

To illustrate the power of matching survey responses with data from other sources, consider the following three cases on sales performance, retention, and the impact of managers on the bottom line.

Case study #1: Sales performance. Analyzing sales data variation over time, location, and salespeople provides information on trends and individual differences. However, such analysis does not provide the reason for those differences. In order to get actionable insights that can be applied to increase sales performance, companies need to understand how their people and processes impact sales. When Frito-Lay was faced with higher turnover than it wanted among its route sales reps (RSRs), it sought to understand the role of compensation versus other factors in driving turnover.

To get the desired insights, Frito-Lay conducted a study of the design of the RSR job, which included surveys of the RSRs and separate surveys of their supervisors matched with individual RSR performance data (Levenson and Faber, 2009). The RSR surveys were used to determine that there was a positive relationship between prior sales experience and sales performance. The supervisor surveys were used to collect ratings of the RSRs on three facets of job performance—sales tasks, driving/delivery tasks, merchandising tasks—and match those to RSR sales performance. That led to important insights regarding the barriers to improved sales performance on high-volume versus low-volume routes and a redesign of the high volume routes. Without the matching of the supervisor surveys to the RSR performance data, identifying the barriers to improved performance and validating the route redesign would not have been possible.

Case study #2: Retention. Retention of key talent is important for any organization looking to maintain a competitive advantage. Questions about intention to turnover are commonly found on many employee surveys, and they have been shown to be predictive of actual turnover in the scientific literature. Yet despite the research evidence, key decision makers in organizations often want validation that such questions can be linked to turnover in their organizations. This can be especially true in organizations that use intention to turnover data as a trigger for taking action to reduce actual turnover.

When PwC conducted a study of retention of its key talent, it gained deep insights into the drivers of intention to turnover that the firm used to implement change and reduce actual turnover (Levenson, Fenlon, and Benson, 2010). The primary insights came from a behavioral model that used statistical analysis to weigh the different factors contributing to turnover intention; see chapter seven for details on statistical behavioral modeling using employee survey data. Yet despite the depth of those insights, additional validation of the data was desired. So the firm tracked actual turnover for its employees and matched it back to the survey responses. Doing so revealed a strong relationship between individual employees' stated intention to turnover and their actual turnover behavior. This validated the results of the turnover model and supported the firm's later decisions to use employee surveys and behavioral modeling to investigate other issues beyond turnover.

Case study #3: Impact of managers on the bottom line. Managerial competency models are used in most large organizations and can be effective tools for communicating the importance of behaviors the organization wants to promote throughout the leadership ranks. Organizations devote extensive resources to developing and implementing competency frameworks, including common use of 360 evaluations. Yet despite all the attention put into managerial competencies, there is little published scientific evidence that they make a contribution to organizational performance and the bottom line.

When a consumer products company wanted to test whether there was a link between the competency model for managers in its manufacturing plants and operational performance, it turned to an employee survey matched with operational performance data for each plant (Levenson, Van der Stede, and Cohen, 2006). The survey addressed key aspects of the relationship between managers and the competency framework, including their understanding of it, how they felt about its fairness, and the extent to which they were mentored on it. Those data were used to measure the impact of the competency system on individual performance and showed that mentoring had a positive impact. A further analysis of data aggregated to the plant level showed a positive impact on organizational performance of having more high-competency managers at a site.

Summary of Key Points from This Chapter:

- ✓ Matching survey responses with other data can show a link to business performance.

- ✓ For employees like salespeople with clear performance metrics, the matching is best when it can happen at the individual employee level.

- ✓ Keeping the identity of survey respondents anonymous is the best way to ensure that they will feel comfortable answering all questions honestly. With anonymous survey responses, however, matching with data from other sources can take place only at the group level.

- ✓ Ensuring anonymity or confidentiality is needed to encourage the survey respondents to be honest and forthcoming about sensitive issues.

- ✓ Be careful to not ask for extremely detailed demographic information that could be used to reverse engineer privacy controls and reveal people's identities.

part three

SURVEY ANALYSIS, INTERPRETATION, AND ACTION TAKING

chapter six

KISS

THE POWER AND PITFALLS OF SIMPLICITY

The old adage "keep it simple stupid" (or KISS, for short) applies just as much, if not more so, to designing and administering employee surveys. Employees don't wake up in the morning wanting to be surveyed. Managers don't dream of the data they are going to receive from their employees.

Employee surveys typically measure many different types of constructs (sets of questions that together measure a single concept), and the results have to be communicated back to stakeholders who are very busy and often demand simple messages to focus and act on. The survey needs to be as straightforward and uncomplicated as possible to ensure the greatest buy-in, response rates, and follow-up actions. The use of red (high urgency) / yellow (medium urgency) / green (low urgency) color coding to highlight areas of importance for executives to focus on is one example of techniques used to provide a simple roadmap to a busy audience; see chapter eight for further discussion of this approach. It is also common to group questions by topic for easier-to-understand feedback; for example, compensation and benefits, leadership, learning/training/development, and diversity. These and other practices can effectively simplify a complex survey without compromising any of the objectives.

Taking the simplification one step further, some survey administrators will create a composite index consisting of the average of all the questions on a topic. This practice is closely related to the development of constructs; see chapter four for more details on constructs. However, there is an important difference between creating constructs based on statistical analysis of survey questions and this practice used by some popular survey vendors. They use composite indexes of different question types to present an overall measurement of employee engagement or something similar. Yet because the questions measure very different things, there is no statistical basis for combining them together in one index. These indexes obscure critical information and can lead you to focus on the wrong measurements.

In this chapter I discuss the **tradeoffs of using composite indexes of dissimilar questions**, using examples that are common today. Recommendations on how to interpret the real information in these indexes and how to maximize the relevance of the different parts of an index are provided.

Like a stock market index, only different. Creating a composite index of employee sentiment is similar to creating a stock market index. Indexes provide simple ways of summarizing the performance of a large number of stocks. For example, in the United States the S&P 500 summarizes the performance of the largest stocks, the NASDAQ provides a snapshot of how the technology sector is performing, and the small-cap Russell 2000 index focuses on smaller publicly traded companies. These snapshots are important for understanding broad market trends and commonalities across many companies. Yet they mask enormous differences in the performance of individual stocks. They help with understanding the big picture of factors that affect all stocks but are almost useless when it comes to understanding the performance of individual stocks.

Composite indexes of dissimilar employee survey questions have similar strengths and weaknesses. They can easily summarize employee sentiment over a dissimilar set of questions. Yet they reveal nothing about differences in individual survey questions unless you focus on both the index and the individual questions. This is similar in the stock case to using the information from both the index and individual stock prices when making investment decisions, which is always a sound approach.

The main feature that distinguishes composite indexes of survey questions from constructs is the similarity of the questions that are combined together. A construct uses questions that are deliberately worded to be similar to ensure that a single idea is being measured precisely and accurately. For example, the following questions can be used to measure the construct of shared understanding about a team's objectives and approaches for accomplishing them:

- ✓ We have a shared understanding of what we are trying to accomplish on my team.
- ✓ There is agreement about our priorities on my team.
- ✓ There is an agreed way of getting the work done on my team.
- ✓ People on my team do not agree on what is really important. (*reversed*)

Alternatively, consider the following questions that can be used to measure task-based trust on a team:

- ✓ Team members always do what they say they will do.
- ✓ The people on my team are reliable in their work.
- ✓ Team members believe that others on our team will follow through on their commitments.

The Resources section provides additional construct examples for intention to turnover, supervisor support, and organizational commitment.

A composite index, in contrast, purposefully combines together dissimilar questions to provide a summary of employee sentiment that otherwise could be difficult to discern. This approach has grown in popularity in recent years with the increasing emphasis on measuring employee engagement. Consider the following questions, which are examples that have been used as parts of a composite engagement score by consulting companies with large client lists:

- ✓ I have the materials and equipment to do my work.
- ✓ At work my opinion seems to count.
- ✓ I am satisfied with the recognition I receive from my immediate supervisor for doing a good job.
- ✓ I rarely think about looking for a new job with another company.

All of these questions provide dissimilar insights into important aspects of the employment relationship: resource support, two-way communication, feedback/ recognition, and intention to stay.

When creating constructs, statistical analysis is used to validate that the individual questions measure the same thing. Though individual questions might seem different from each other, the statistics show that each person who responds positively to one of the questions in a construct tends to respond the same way to all the questions in the construct, and vice versa. In contrast, the composite score is used as a summary measure even though the individual questions might measure quite distinct and separate things. There is nothing inherently wrong with doing this; however, it is important to keep in mind that an overall summary score for a category that is constructed from dissimilar questions can obscure important differences among the questions in the category.

For example, consider a "leadership" category consisting of multiple questions including one on communication and one on coaching. One manager might score high on communication and medium on coaching, while the opposite might be the case for another manager. Because of the averaging, both managers could have the exact same overall composite score, even though the individual items reveal different strengths and weaknesses across individual managers. Note that this could not be the case for individual survey questions that are statistically proven to be part of a single construct: if questions A and B are both part of a valid construct, then (virtually) everyone scoring high, medium, or low on A will score similarly on B—that is the point of the statistical validation of the construct.

As discussed in chapter three, the importance of the different items in the engagement index listed above will vary across people, roles, and business units. Resource support varies significantly across the enterprise, depending on what is viewed as strategically important, how skillful local managers are in arguing for support, and budget allocations. Two-way communication can be more important in certain types of roles—those requiring more autonomy and independent decision making—than in other roles and can also be subject to the skills and notions of local managers. Feedback is important in all roles, yet there are significant differences in people's preferences for how communication occurs. Intention to stay (or intention to turnover) is highly variable across people, in addition to having differential strategic importance across roles; in roles where replacements are easy to find and time to productivity for new people in the role is low, high turnover does not pose a threat to productivity or organizational effectiveness. Thus the scores for the separate items in this index can vary substantially across individual employees, teams, units, and managers even though the overall composite score might be similar.

The composite index as greatest common denominator. Given these differences, what does the composite index score represent? Combining together very different questions in a single numerical index is often the same as constructing a general affect measure—a measure of how satisfied or content the survey respondent is. For example, consider the items that comprise Gallup's engagement index:

- ✓ I know what is expected of me at work.
- ✓ I have the materials and equipment I need to do my work right.
- ✓ At work, I have the opportunity to do what I do best every day.
- ✓ In the last seven days, I have received recognition or praise for doing good work.

✓ My supervisor, or someone at work, seems to care about me as a person.

✓ There is someone at work who encourages my development.

✓ At work, my opinions seem to count.

✓ The mission/purpose of my company makes me feel my job is important.

✓ My associates (fellow employees) are committed to doing quality work.

✓ I have a best friend at work.

✓ In the last six months, someone at work has talked to me about my progress.

✓ This last year, I have had opportunities at work to learn and grow.

The items in the Gallup engagement index clearly measure a wide variety of things that are quite different in many ways. Yet Gallup uses the index as a composite measure of employee engagement, and claims both a strong link to business performance and that the 12-item index is statistically valid. However, in a rigorous statistical analysis published in the *Journal of Applied Psychology*, a topnotch scientific journal, Harter, Schmidt, and Hayes (2002) used Gallup's own data to demonstrate that a single job satisfaction question has the exact same statistical relationship with business unit performance as the 12-item employee engagement index (table five, p. 274). How can this be?

The answer lies in a mathematical concept you may recall from middle school: the greatest common denominator. In order for Gallup's twelve items to be considered a cohesive index, the index has to differentiate people based on how they respond to the entire set of questions. The diversity of the questions at first glance seems to be a strength because the index touches on so many different parts of the employment relationship, yet that apparent strength is actually a mirage. The index can only differentiate people based on how positive versus neutral versus negative they are across the complete set of questions. As the analysis with Gallup's own data shows, it turns out that that differentiation is no different than general satisfaction with the job and working environment. Job satisfaction is the greatest common denominator across these questions, and there is no statistical added value provided by combining all the questions together into a single index. Asking the single job satisfaction question is much less burdensome and straightforward.

It is worth noting that, in a strictly technical sense, the Gallup index does meet one of the criteria outlined at the beginning of this section: a set of questions grouped together with a statistical basis for doing so. The technical issue is that the only way the statistics work is because Gallup excludes multiple questions from the different categories in the engagement index—multiple questions on intention to turnover, on supervisor support, on development support, and so on. If the excluded questions were included and the statistical analysis was repeated, what would emerge would not be a single statistically valid index, but multiple distinct constructs. This is an example of how the statistical results of a factor analysis can be biased by including only one question from many different constructs.

Even more importantly, just because Gallup's twelve items are indistinguishable from a single job satisfaction question when used together, that does NOT mean they have no independently valuable information. The reality is quite the opposite: many of the individual questions in the index have high value in terms of insights provided into employee attitudes about their jobs, careers, and work environment. Problems arise when they are combined in a single index and the organization focuses principally on the index versus the individual questions.

If the desire is to focus on some of the separate constructs represented by individual questions, every single question should be considered on its own merits and not included in an employee survey just because a survey vendor like Gallup or its clients have used them in the past. For example, the following two questions are reasonable single-item versions of established constructs:

- ✓ Resource support: "I have the materials and equipment I need to do my work right."

- ✓ Feedback: "In the last seven days, I have received recognition or praise for doing good work."

This next set of five questions provides acceptable examples of single items that are related to established constructs. They could be used "as is" to partially measure the indicated constructs but would be improved by rewording or pairing with multiple questions on the same topic:

- ✓ Goal setting: "I know what is expected of me at work."
- ✓ Development support: "There is someone at work who encourages my development."
- ✓ Learning: "This last year, I have had opportunities at work to learn and grow."
- ✓ Trust/team support: "My associates (fellow employees) are committed to doing quality work."
- ✓ Job fit: "At work, I have the opportunity to do what I do best every day."

This final set of five questions is somewhat related to established constructs, but only loosely. It would be advisable to use questions from the established constructs instead.

- ✓ "At work, my opinions seem to count": If the employee has lots of opinions on irrelevant or non–work-related matters, what is measured by this question would have no relationship to relevant work-related issues. It would be better to focus the question on opportunities to contribute suggestions or ideas for improving work processes or the work environment.

✓ "My supervisor, or someone at work, seems to care about me as a person": This question would be okay for measuring a humane workplace, but it runs the risk of confounding the supervisor relationship, which is central to motivation and intention to turnover, with relationships with colleagues, who may have no influence over the employee's fate. Better to use well-established questions that focus on the relationship with supervisor, such as "my supervisor is willing to help me when I need a special favor" or "my supervisor really cares about my well-being."

✓ "The mission/purpose of my company makes me feel my job is important": Identifying with the organization's mission is a type of job or organization fit, which is better measured with more specific job fit or organization fit questions.

✓ "I have a best friend at work": Whether people develop close friendships at work has more to do with serendipity and personal inclinations to socialize with colleagues after work hours than anything within the organization's control. The organizational commitment construct uses language that is similar in tone but focuses more specifically on how the individual relates to the organization, not the existence of a friendship that may be only tangentially related to broader feelings of attachment to the workplace. Examples of questions from the organization commitment construct include "I do not feel like 'part of the family' at this company" and "I feel a strong sense of belonging to my company."

✓ "In the last six months, someone at work has talked to me about my progress": Not only is this question vague about who is doing the communicating, but it doesn't even specify if the conversation happened professionally or was totally botched. Better to focus on whether the respondent feels he or she received helpful feedback about performance or career progression.

Given the prevalence of Gallup and other consulting companies' employee engagement indexes and the large number of clients that use them, at this point you might be wondering if I support using any type of employee engagement index. The answer is yes, but the index has to be defined appropriately to measure what we mean by employee engagement. Rather than combining dissimilar questions into a single index, the outcome should be a well-defined measure of engagement that is not the same thing as job satisfaction or another general measure of employee affect.

For example, a recent contribution from the research literature was provided by Porath, Spreitzer, Gibson, and

Garnett (2011), among others. They propose a measure of "thriving" at work, consisting of two parts: learning and vitality. These authors use both statistics and logic to argue persuasively that these measures of learning and vitality together provide a good snapshot of how much employees are thriving at work. Of course, there are other ways of conceptualizing what employee engagement is, and thriving is just one approach. The main point is that the item or items you choose, whatever they are, should be clean and straightforward to measure and interpret, like the learning or vitality approaches. You should try to avoid using a grab-bag of only loosely related items that raise more questions than insights. If you do use such a grab-bag, be aware that you likely are taking a complicated path to measuring something simple like job satisfaction, which could be addressed directly with fewer questions.

Summary of Key Points from This Chapter

- ✔ Composite indexes are good at capturing general employee moods.

- ✔ For deeper insights, focus on the components of the index, not the aggregated index score.

- ✔ Employee engagement is best measured by focusing on specific employee attitude(s) such as intention to turnover, job satisfaction, thriving, commitment, and so on. Combining multiple measures into a single index usually yields no different insights than a single question on job satisfaction.

chapter seven

THE BIG PICTURE
WHAT, HOW, WHY, AND WHO
OF STATISTICAL MODELING

In order for a survey to deliver actionable insights, it has to provide guidance on what measures matter most and why. Many of the deepest insights from employee surveys are available only through statistical modeling: the social science research foundation that has provided most of the current insights into the factors driving employee motivation and behavior. Yet statistical modeling is rarely used to analyze employee surveys even though the techniques are well developed and relatively easy to apply. In this chapter I review **statistical modeling** and who best to engage to do the work.

Statistical models: the basics. A multivariate statistical model identifies an outcome of interest (the dependent factor or variable) and a set of potential factors that influence or drive the outcome (independent factors or variables). Common outcomes of interest include intention to turnover, commitment, and job satisfaction. Figure one is an example of a statistical model of employee intention to turnover or engagement:

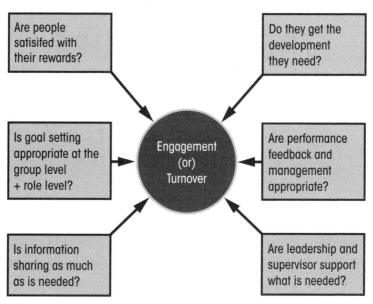

figure one **Statistical model of employee intention to turnover or engagement**

In this model the dependent variable is engagement or turnover. The independent variables are:

- ✓ Pay/rewards satisfaction
- ✓ Development support
- ✓ Performance feedback
- ✓ Supervisor/organization support

✓ Information sharing/communication

✓ Goal setting/fairness

Statistical analysis of a multivariate model tells us which independent factors have the strongest impact on the dependent factor. The statistical analysis results can provide clear guidance on the factors with the strongest impact on the outcome of interest. If you want to know which levers will have the biggest impact for improving employee engagement, retention, and so on, statistical modeling is the most powerful tool available for identifying those levers.

The techniques used to analyze statistical models include regression analysis, ANOVA, and maximum likelihood estimation. The good news is that deriving the insights from statistical models does not require knowing how to interpret the dense and difficult-to-understand results that are generated by the typical statistical software package. There are ample resources available to help externally, and often internally—people whose jobs are to interpret and present the results of statistical analyses in a way that is easily accessible.

Statistical analysis of the model in figure one would tell you which independent variables are significantly related to turnover and which have the strongest relationships. For example, the analysis results summarized for a nonstatistician audience might look like the example in table one.

Factors impacting intention to turnover	Strength of the relationship (how much each factor reduces intention to turnover)
Pay/rewards satisfaction	+3
Development support	+1
Performance feedback	0
Supervisor/organization support	+3
Information sharing/ communication	+2
Goal setting/fairness	+3

table one **Intention to turnover analysis results summarized for nonstatistician audience**

The initial output of statistical modeling is usually presented in a highly technical way designed only for people who have training in statistics. Table one, in contrast, reports the results in a way that anyone without training in statistics should be able to grasp easily. A larger number indicates a stronger relationship between the factor and intention to turnover. A number greater than zero indicates a positive relationship, while a number less than zero indicates a negative relationship. The size and sign are determined by the statistical analysis results.

The results in table one indicate that pay/rewards satisfaction, supervisor/organization support, and goal setting/fairness have the biggest impact on intention to turnover: improvements in these factors will lead to the biggest reductions. Information sharing/communication is a close runner-up: an improvement in this factor will also reduce intention to turnover but by not as much as the three strongest factors. Improvements in development support also have an impact on intention to turnover, but the improvements are not as strong as for information sharing/communication, and are much weaker than the three leading factors. Improvements in performance feedback, in contrast to all the other factors, have no impact on intention to turnover for the group of people who took this survey.

It is important to note that the strength of the relationship between each factor included in a statistical model and the dependent variable is *not* related to the average value of the factor. Table two adds to table one the average response values:

Factors impacting intention to turnover	Strength of the relationship (how much each factor reduces intention to turnover)	Percent agree (or strongly agree)
Pay/rewards satisfaction	+3	46%
Development support	+1	80%
Performance feedback	0	70%
Supervisor/organization support	+3	73%
Information sharing/ communication	+2	68%
Goal setting/fairness	+3	39%

table two **Intention to turnover analysis results with average response values included**

The three factors in table two that have the biggest impact on reducing intention to turnover have quite different average values, ranging from goal setting/fairness with 39 percent agree on the low end to supervisor/organization support with 73 percent on the high end. Despite the widely varying percent agree for the three factors, the statistical model results indicate that the same improvement in any of the three factors—for example 10 percentage points higher for percent agree—would yield the same reduction in intention to turnover despite the vastly different starting points for each factor in the survey sample.

This example underlines the importance of focusing on statistical models and not just average responses or percent agree for the factors measured in a survey. It also helps put in perspective the problem with common practice today for sharing employee survey results. When organizations widely distribute the average responses to employee survey questions, the people reading the results are drawn first and foremost to looking at how "good" the organization, unit, or group did for each item or construct, comparing percent agree values like in column three in table two above. To make this a more useful exercise, the insights from statistical modeling are needed so that the people reviewing the results can put them into context. Without that context, the focus too often is on low percent agree scores, while ignoring information on which factors are most likely to lead to improvements in the outcome you care about (turnover, engagement, etc.). Statistical modeling helps provides the answers to the questions: "How do we make sense of all these survey data?"

and "What should we focus on to have the biggest impact on employee attitudes and motivation?" This is why there is no substitute for the depth of the insights provided by a statistical model.

Choose the right survey vendor with statistical modeling in mind. By now you hopefully are convinced of the importance of doing statistical modeling with your employee survey data. But how should you do it—who should take the lead? This is where the choice of the vendor that conducts the survey becomes very important.

Deciding to use survey vendors just because they have long lists of "A-level" clients is like putting the cart before the horse. Even big, successful, industry-leading companies do not always use the best judgment when choosing survey vendors: business is often won on the basis of sales skills, not value added. When the survey vendor's technical expertise is part of the criteria, the focus is usually on reporting the results and degree of customization. The vendor's ability to conduct and report statistical analyses in an accessible way is usually not high on the list of criteria and often isn't even a consideration. That is a lost opportunity for maximizing the value and insights from employee surveys.

When looking for the right survey vendor, you should consider the direct value they will provide in terms of responsiveness to your needs, customization, reporting, and ease of use. You should not choose them on the basis of a stock list of survey items; see the caution against external benchmarking in chapter eight. Choose them on the basis of the value they can add to analyzing your data and helping you to make sense of it, particularly through statistical modeling.

Giving higher priority to statistical modeling when selecting and engaging with survey vendors is easier than you may think and should not lead to a big disruption in the vendor-client relationship. If you have internal organization development experts in your organization, they should already know quite well how to use surveys for statistical modeling. Your OD colleagues can assist in specifying the models to be run, working with the survey vendor on how to run them and present the results, and, if necessary, even running the statistical models themselves.

Regardless of whether you already have that kind of survey expertise internally in your organization, your survey vendor should have it. Many of the technical experts who work in the survey vendor industry come from research backgrounds. When vendors sell a particular approach to measuring and understanding employee engagement, motivation, retention, and so on, that approach is often based on statistical models estimated on other companies' data. What the vendor often fails to do, however, is encourage additional statistical modeling using the data collected from your employees. That is the main source of the lost opportunity.

Why don't vendors promote statistical modeling for each client they work with and engagement they work on? For one thing, people in sales roles for the vendors often do not deeply understand the nuances of statistical modeling and so cannot directly address the pros and cons of including that as part of the contracted services. Second, when vendors develop stock sets of survey questions based on statistical models run on previous data, they can sell access to the questions and a benchmarking database at low cost. This has an appeal to business leaders who like benchmarking but in reality provides low value added; see the discussion in chapter eight for further details. The greatest value added and insights come from specifying and estimating separately the right statistical model for each distinct set of employees.

It can be difficult to figure out where to hold the line on making the survey effort more complicated. Though the greatest insights often are found when you do statistical modeling for each distinct group of employees, there is a significant cost-benefit tradeoff that has to be factored in. Every time you do a separate statistical model or estimation there is a lot of customized work involved. Recognizing the significant time, effort, and expense needed to do each statistical model, most survey experts emphasize the efficiency of using their existing models.

What is needed is a more balanced approach. Rather than make the decision for you, your survey vendor should engage you in the discussion of the pros and cons of creating and running statistical models for different groups of employees. Even if you decide to use only one model, estimating the model separately for different groups of employees can lead to important insights into the factors that matter for each group, such as pay, workload/work-life balance, the importance of professional development, and so on. The large differences in experience people in different roles have should make you cautious about using a global statistical model for all employees in your organization and across all of your survey vendor's clients. A little customization can go a long way toward generating truly meaningful and actionable insights. These issues are further addressed in the next chapter on the value and insights available from benchmarking internally versus externally.

Summary of Key Points from This Chapter:

- ✔ Analyzing average responses to a survey question or correlations between questions are the most common ways of engaging with survey data, yet they are rarely actionable on their own.

- ✔ Statistical models of employee attitudes yields the deepest insights into the factors that matter for employee engagement, retention, and so on.

- ✔ The results of statistical modeling should be presented in a way that all stakeholders can interpret and should not require advanced statistical training to understand.

- ✔ Survey vendors' and internal experts' statistical skills should be better leveraged for running statistical models using employee survey data.

chapter eight

REACHING CONCLUSIONS
BENCHMARKING AND STATISTICAL VERSUS MEANINGFUL DIFFERENCES

Leaders love to benchmark because doing so can be critically important for strategy. Benchmarking tells us how our prices, quality, customer service, customer loyalty, margins, market share, and profitability measure up to our competitors. So of course benchmarking on employee attitudes is always a good thing, right? Unfortunately, not necessarily. Benchmarking employee survey responses to external data is at best mildly informative; at worst it can lead to misdirection and wasted effort, which can undermine employee engagement—the opposite of the outcome we want to occur. Benchmarking internally often leads to deeper and more actionable insights.

Whether you benchmark internally or externally, if you see a difference in the data you also need a way of determining if the difference is meaningful. Statistical tests provide one way of determining if a difference is real. Practical significance is more important than statistical significance but also is more subjective and harder to gauge. Determining what data is worth acting on is part science, part art, and part logic: you need to understand what the data mean in context to determine the best course to take based on them.

This chapter addresses **making comparisons**: comparing survey results to benchmark data and determining if a perceived difference is meaningful.

Benchmarking externally. Employee psychology is a tricky and multifaceted thing. There are a large number of factors that combine to create satisfaction or dissatisfaction at work. Differences in compensation design, internal career paths, management processes, supervisor quality, development opportunities, and more combine to create unique organizational cultures and work experiences across organizations. Oracle, Microsoft, Google, IBM, and Apple are all in the tech industry and have employees who work in both hardware and software. Yet their cultures, employee value propositions, and internal career paths are quite distinct. Comparing the answers to similarly worded questions across these organizations without any regard for the different contexts of the employees that answered them is misguided. This is why benchmarking survey items across organizations, even within the same industry, usually is not very useful. It can help overcome complacency if used to encourage leaders to address issues that are festering unattended. However, it can be counterproductive if used as a rallying cry to "beat" your competitors with a goal of attaining higher levels of agreement with specific survey items.

The deepest insights possible from your employee survey come from understanding how the various parts of what you offer to your employees combine together as a package. You may be low on pay satisfaction relative to your competitors but higher on opportunities for development and supervisor support. Faced with benchmark data like this, what is the conclusion you should reach about whether to try to close the gap on pay satisfaction or double down and pay even more attention to development and managerial behaviors? The answer is you cannot know what to act on simply by comparing average responses across survey items. Instead, use your data to model the drivers of employee satisfaction, intention to turnover, and so on, and compare how important each of the different elements is using statistical analysis. These models are standard in social science research, and many HR analytics experts, whether in your organization or employed by your survey vendor, are well equipped to apply them to the data you already have in hand. All you have to do is ask. See chapter seven for further discussion of statistical modeling and using survey experts to help you.

If you take this approach, you will get deeper insights into the real drivers of employee attitudes and inoculate

your organization against a common misguided practice: setting arbitrary targets (percent agree) on specific
survey questions as measures of whether things are going well. Leaders and consultants love to use a stoplight
analogy to create red/yellow/green indicators for survey
responses as a way of focusing attention on areas that
score relatively low: red for areas of urgent need, yellow
for areas to be addressed but not as urgently, and green
for areas that do not need to be addressed. Usually there
is no scientific justification for classifying a survey item as
red/yellow/green simply because it might have a lower
percentage of people who agree unless that conclusion
is tied to a specific statistical model showing that the item
in question is important for driving employee attitudes.

For example, pay satisfaction scores are typically low
for all employees. Consider two jobs—machine operator
and senior executive—and a model of intention to turnover. The percent agree for pay satisfaction for the machine operators is 78 percent, while for senior executives
it is 66 percent. Does this mean that dissatisfaction with
pay is more likely to drive senior executives to leave than it
is for machine operators? Not necessarily. In fact, because
frontline employees like machine operators are paid at
substantially lower levels than senior executives, differences among them in pay and in pay satisfaction can be
more important drivers of retention than for senior executives. For the senior executives, in contrast, their power
and status in the organization may be more than enough
to get them to stay even if they would like greater pay. For
both groups, the only way to be certain how important pay

is relative to other parts of the job and opportunities at the organization is to run the statistical model separately for each group. The results of doing the analysis might look like table three:

Factors impacting intention to turnover by employee group	Strength of the relationship (how much each factor reduces intention to turnover)	Percent agree (or strongly agree)
For machine operators:		
Pay/rewards satisfaction	+3	78%
Factor B ...	...	...
Factor C ...	...	...
For executives:		
Pay/rewards satisfaction	+1	66%
Factor B ...	...	...
Factor C ...	...	...

table three **Intention to turnover analyzed separately for different employee groups**

The results in the table three example also illustrate another key point from the discussion of statistical modeling in chapter seven: just because the executives in this sample score much lower in pay/rewards satisfaction, that does not mean that trying to improve their satisfaction with higher compensation will have a big impact on their retention. Even though the machine operators score higher than the executives in pay/rewards satisfaction, making improvements on that front will have a much bigger impact on their retention than a comparable improvement would have on the retention of executives.

The key issue here, which is well known to social science researchers, is that you cannot tell from the mean responses how important a survey question is for driving employee behavior. You need behavioral models that are estimated using statistical analysis to tell you the importance of specific factors. For example, one group of employees might score lower than their peers in other organizations on work-life balance, but that does not necessarily mean that they will be less engaged or more likely to leave your organization. You have to consider the entire package of what employees get from working for your organization and the contribution of each element of the package to motivation, engagement, productivity, and retention. Only statistical analysis of behavioral models can enable that.

Benchmarking internally. While it is hard to derive actionable insights when benchmarking employee survey data externally, it is easier when benchmarking internally. Important insights can be learned by benchmarking against other jobs internally and tracking key metrics over time.

The main benefit of doing internal comparisons is that everyone works for the same organization. This means that many of the factors that create differences in employees' experiences across organizations are held constant: the types of products and services provided to customers, business strategy, organization design and processes, HR systems and policies, and so on. Of course there are differences in the experiences employees have depending on their role/occupation, location, and job level. So internal benchmarking across employees should focus as much as possible on apples-to-apples comparisons: people in the same function, business unit, or similar roles.

The most actionable insights available from internal benchmarking are comparisons or trends over time for a group of employees. If a group of survey questions and constructs (sets of questions that together measure a single concept) are measured consistently over time, you can track changes to see whether scores are increasing or decreasing. This type of comparison provides the cleanest, most straightforward way of monitoring whether something might have changed in a way that is significant and potentially actionable.

For example, suppose your organization recently went through a difficult period of poor business performance and low morale. After working through a transition and turnaround phase, you want to use your annual employee survey to determine whether things have improved sufficiently. If you have enough data from before the difficult period to measure a decline in employee sentiment on measures like job satisfaction, pay satisfaction, career satisfaction, and organizational commitment, you could look to see if those measures have improved. You may have a hypothesis that the measured levels (percent agree) should return to levels similar to one or two years prior to the business downturn, and you could test for that. Of course, you need a well-specified behavioral model for why that should take place. Without such a model, even if you observe differences before versus after the difficult period, you cannot necessarily conclude that action should be taken to address any potential "problem" with differing employee attitudes.

Don't lose sight of both statistical and practical significance. It is widely known, even among people without advanced training in statistics, that you have to be careful when deciding whether there are real differences when comparing two numbers. This is why "lying with statistics" is such a commonly used phrase: it is easy to get confused about what makes for meaningful differences.

The important point is that there are both statistical and practical differences. Statistical differences are mathematically determined and follow very specific, clear rules. Practical differences are a bit trickier to nail down and require using a combination of both logic and judgment. To make the distinction clear, first consider the statistical issues.

Looking for statistically significant differences. When statisticians test for differences, they look at the "confidence interval." The confidence interval is an amount around a number, plus or minus, that is used to determine if that number is statistically different from another number. Let's say we conduct a survey and find out that 55 percent of the respondents respond favorably (agree or strongly agree) to a question about job satisfaction. Now suppose that we want to know whether that 55 percent can be considered different from 50 percent, the figure from last year. This means conducting a statistical test of whether 55 percent is different from 50 percent. Of course those two numbers are different, but the first question is whether the difference is statistically significant in this context.

Statistically speaking, we need to know the confidence interval around the estimate that 55 percent agree on job satisfaction. This is an estimate because surveys never get 100-percent response rates, and many surveys are administered to less than 100 percent of the target population. Consequently, survey measurements are estimates of what the complete population would look like if we could collect data from every single person. The confidence interval tells us if there is enough data to conclude that a difference is large enough to be considered real or not large enough and thus potentially due to chance.

If the sample is small, the confidence interval will be large—it could be as high as plus or minus 7 percent, for example, meaning ranging from 48 percent to 62 percent or even larger. With a confidence interval that wide, we cannot conclude that 55 percent is statistically different from 50 percent; the difference in the numbers we are testing—55 percent versus 50 percent—could be due to random variation. Random variation is more of an issue in small samples: we cannot know for sure if the differences are due to something real that applies to a much larger group of people or to the luck of the draw in who responded to the survey or the people selected from the overall population to be included in the survey sample.

Confidence intervals for larger samples are small and could be as low as plus or minus 2 percent in this case—for example, meaning ranging from 53 percent to 57 percent or even smaller. With a confidence interval that narrow, we can conclude that 55 percent is statistically different from 50 percent, and that random variation is not creating perceived differences that aren't actually real.

This distinction between statistically significant versus not significant differences is important to keep in mind when tracking employee survey data over time. Executives who monitor operational metrics are used to looking for minor deviations and can be "trigger happy" with employee survey data: when they see a small change in survey responses they can prematurely conclude that something has to be acted upon, whether celebrated (positive change) or corrected (negative change). If a change is not statistically significant, the immediate response should be to not take action and to seek additional information to inform decision making.

Looking for meaningful differences. Even if we conclude that 55 percent agree for job satisfaction this year is statistically significantly different from 50 percent last year, there remains the issue of practical or meaningful significance. When we see the percent agree shift by 5 percentage points for job satisfaction from one year to the next on a survey, how much importance should we put behind that number? The answer is it depends on the context.

Suppose this was a turnaround situation where engagement scores had fallen sharply and then started to trend back up last year. Three years ago, before the business problems, job satisfaction was at 70 percent, around where it had been for a number of years; in the five years to that point it ranged from 67 percent to 73 percent, with the last reading at 70 percent before sales fell dramatically. After the sales drop, measured job satisfaction two years ago fell to 40 percent in the middle of a large layoff. One year later, after sales had stabilized at a lower level, and there were no additional layoffs, job satisfaction rebounded to 50 percent.

In this context, 55 percent agree currently for job satisfaction is simultaneously positive and negative. Given the long-term history of the site, it might be reasonable to expect job satisfaction to eventually return to the historical average around 70 percent. Viewed this way, a reading of 55 percent is far short of the goal and potentially negative. Consider further the slowdown in job satisfaction growth from plus 10 percentage points 2 years ago to plus 5 percentage points this year. The slowdown could be further evidence that improvements are waning and we should worry about the slowdown.

On the other hand, the large layoffs and reorganization at the site could mean the situation today is different and won't go back to what it was before. If workloads and job responsibilities increased, morale might stay depressed relative to the historical readings; if so, a current reading of 55 percent might be close to the maximum to be expected. Viewed this way, a tapered off rebound in job satisfaction might indicate the current management team is doing the best that it can under more difficult circumstances. So whether the change from 50 percent to 55 percent for job satisfaction is viewed as positive or negative depends on the context and previous history.

Alternatively, consider a site with no reorganization and historical turnover consistently 25 to 30 percent annually. The job satisfaction scores at the site bounce around a bit historically, falling in the 45 to 55 percent range over a 7-year period. The local leadership suspects that a change in personnel from one year to the next is largely responsible for the movement in job satisfaction because none of the work systems or management processes have changed. In this context, how should a reading of 55 percent be viewed? Given the site history, without additional information a logical conclusion is the year-over-year change from 50 percent to 55 percent is normal statistical "noise"; it is not a meaningful change.

This further illustrates the importance of understanding the context and history behind a survey measurement so that you can determine whether an observed change or difference is meaningful. Doing so is important to ensure that management does not rationalize away lower scores while ensuring that the appropriate caution is taken when interpreting and deciding to act on changes in scores.

Summary of Key Points from This Chapter:

✔ External benchmarking to data from other organizations is widely practiced, but not very informative or actionable. More actionable insights are available via internal benchmarking.

✔ Benchmarking is most informative when it is an apples-to-apples comparison of similar roles and work settings. Comparisons of larger, more diverse groups of employees are not suitable for identifying meaningful differences between the groups.

✔ The most informative benchmarking is usually for the same group over time.

✔ Before you can conclude that two benchmarking numbers are different, you have to consider both statistical significance and practical significance. If the data do not support a difference that is both statistically and practically significant, then it may be due to random factors and almost never is actionable without more data or other information to corroborate the conclusions.

chapter nine

MOVING FORWARD

REPORTING AND TAKING ACTION

Peter Drucker is famously quoted as saying, "What gets measured, gets managed." This adage has never been more accurate than today. The reason we conduct employee surveys is to improve management effectiveness. Without the quantifiable data that a survey provides, many people-related issues would suffer from benign neglect or outright indifference.

The flipside holds as well: if you measure something you should be prepared to take action. The act of doing the measurement sends a strong signal to the survey participants and organizational stakeholders that the topics are important for key decision makers. The way the results are shared with the organization can either reinforce or undermine the measurements' importance and affect how the organization takes action.

The idea that surveys can be used as an integral part of organization diagnosis and change is a founding principle of the field of organization development (OD). Many excellent volumes have been written on OD and using surveys to help drive organizational change. In this concluding chapter I draw from the literature on established OD practices to make some observations about **how to use survey reporting to help drive action** in the right direction. For those interested in more details on OD, surveys, and change, good resources include Cummings and Worley (2008), Gallos (2006), Kraut (2006), Anderson (2011), Cheung-Judge and Holbeche (2012), and Kraut (1996).

Tie reporting back to the purpose and desired outcomes for the survey. In chapter one we discussed the importance of being clear about the purpose of the survey, including the desired outcomes. When designing the survey reporting process, first clearly articulate the purpose of the survey. The data used for reporting and the people who receive it should closely align with the purpose and desired actions following survey implementation.

It's been said a number of times in this book that you should avoid overly long surveys. An additional benefit is that shorter, more focused surveys make reporting and appropriate action taking much easier. Reporting is easier because the narrative of the reporting can flow easily from the purpose. Action taking can be limited to one or two main survey objectives.

In contrast, if extraneous questions are included that are tangential to the main objectives, people might take action based on those questions. Once a survey's data are reported back to key stakeholders, it is hard to control how people use the information. The more extraneous data included, the greater the likelihood that someone will take action based on that data. This can happen even if the intent of the extraneous data was information gathering only: you might not see potential action items in extraneous data, but others might. It is better to restrict the survey to narrowly focus on the main objectives.

For example, suppose you designed a survey to measure a change initiative's effectiveness at aligning the organization around a new strategy and customer focus. A stakeholder might want to include tangential questions about career satisfaction and developmental opportunities. If the survey is not too long you could include those questions. However, there are potential risks. Change measurement and developmental opportunities are very distinct and unrelated topics. Including both in the same survey would distract from the main focus, potentially elevating the careers topic higher in people's minds than you want it to be and lowering the change topic's importance. There is further risk that people would assume that the dual focus means that providing better developmental opportunities could improve the effectiveness of the change effort. Yet change often disrupts traditional career paths, so the career data might directly contradict measurements showing a successful change effort, undermining the story of success. It would be better to keep the survey and reporting focused more narrowly on the new strategy and customer focus.

Engage the organization under study as widely and as broadly as possible in the feedback process. If you field a survey, you need to tell people what you found. People are very busy and don't have spare time for filling out surveys. In order to maintain the trust relationship needed to support future survey efforts, you need to find a way to communicate back to the participants something about the results. This does not mean that you share everything from the survey with everyone, but you do need to communicate something about what was learned and, if possible, the actions taken. When people see value in conducting a survey, they feel it was worthwhile to participate.

The data from the survey that you share with the leadership team and key stakeholders usually is more detailed than what you share with the broader organization. More senior people receive the most detail regarding action items to be taken based on the survey. The results can then be leveraged as part of a larger change process. The report for the broader organization usually has more limited details—enough to ensure people understand key learnings from the survey, but not so much that it undermines leadership's action agenda.

When deciding which data to share with the broader organization, including both negative and positive results is important. Sometimes well-meaning people in leadership or HR want to scrub the results to remove negative messages. You should avoid this: if there are negative things happening widely in the organization, most people already know about them. Providing a sanitized set of feedback in these cases will only undermine confidence in the survey process.

A good practice is to form a committee of a cross-section of employees to review the results and help determine how the organization will respond. This is not always practical. However, when it is possible, doing so can increase the quality of the communication and organizational responses to the survey as well as employee buy-in.

Reporting to the broader organization needs to be closely integrated with the actions to be taken. Getting the timing right is critical. If you distribute the broader results too quickly before the leaders are ready with their action agenda, you will greatly diminish change effectiveness. If you wait too long, the organization can lose focus on the topic which also undermines the ability to drive change.

Tailor reporting as needed by role, function, business unit, and so on. Each part of the organization that receives feedback should have results tailored as much as possible. Data reported to a function or business unit often includes the results for that part of the organization, plus the overall organization's results. In some cases, each individual manager receives the data from his or her work group as well.

There are benefits from a consistent process for engaging managers at all levels, but it is important that the managers focus on what is relevant for themselves locally. Depending on the type of work (manufacturing, R&D, distribution, sales, customer service, internal support, etc.), level of employees, education/career path, extent of interdependency among work group members, and so on, the survey questions that are most relevant for the local group can vary quite a bit across the organization. The problem is not having the process in the first place. Instead, the problem often is how the objectives of the process are defined and carried out among heterogeneous work groups.

Preparing managers to interpret and act on the survey data also can be a conduit for training. Using the data feedback process as the platform, managers can be trained on communication, problem solving, and employee engagement. They also can be introduced to the larger topic of diagnosing and improving organizational effectiveness, with the survey data providing one piece of the puzzle. If the goal is to improve organizational performance, the other pieces of the puzzle have to come from data and metrics beyond the employee survey. The managerial training process should emphasize that aspect as well, which further emphasizes the limitations of diagnosing and acting using only the survey data.

Involve key stakeholders early and often in the data collection and analysis process. In order for the survey results to have the biggest impact, the ultimate decision makers have to be involved early on. This is a critical issue: it is easy to get caught up in the survey process and lose sight of how the data will be used to take action and effect change. Effective change leadership comes from engaging the right stakeholders with the survey in the right way at the right time.

One-half of the challenge of a successful survey is designing the right data collection tool. The other half is engaging with the stakeholders who are best positioned to interpret and act on the data.

Effective stakeholder engagement in the process starts at the very beginning, well before the survey launch. First identify which stakeholders are best positioned to use the data to promote change and which stakeholders are best positioned to block action taking on the issues. Both stakeholder groups have to be engaged during the survey development and fielding process so they are not surprised at the end when presented with the results.

The issue is less about publicizing that the survey is taking place; most key stakeholders will know about the survey. The real issue is their involvement and buy-in with the survey objectives and actions to be taken from the results. If you do not engage stakeholders early in the survey process, they cannot be expected to act on the results after receiving them.

Summary of Key Points from This Chapter:

- ✅ Closely tie survey reporting back to the purpose and desired outcomes for the survey.

- ✅ Engage the organization as broadly as possible in the feedback process.

- ✅ Tailor reporting as needed by role, function, business unit, and so on.

- ✅ Involve key stakeholders early and often in the survey process to maximize effective post-survey action taking.

RESOURCES

This section provides sample examples of survey constructs (sets of questions that together measure a single concept) and questions that are mentioned in the book. These examples are not intended to be used as a complete survey. See Fields (2002) for additional survey constructs.

Individually-focused constructs
Development support

- ✓ Developing employee skills is a high priority for supervisors in this firm.

- ✓ We have a good process for mentoring employees.

- ✓ This firm has a good process for identifying employees' development needs.
- ✓ This firm has a good process for developing people.

Goal commitment

- ✓ I am strongly committed to pursuing my performance goals.
- ✓ It is very important to meet my performance goals.
- ✓ Quite frankly, I don't care if I achieve my performance goals (*reversed*).
- ✓ I am willing to put forth a great deal of effort beyond what I'd normally do to achieve my performance goals.

Goal fairness

- ✓ The steps involved in determining my performance goals are fair.
- ✓ The procedures used to set my performance goals are fair.
- ✓ The overall process for setting my performance goals is fair.

Intention to turnover

- ✓ I plan to look outside my company/firm for a new job within the next year.

✓ I often think about quitting my present job.

✓ It is likely that I will quit my job in the next twelve months.

Job satisfaction

✓ Overall, I am satisfied with my job at *<insert name of organization>*.

Mindless work

✓ My job is routine.

✓ My job is boring.

✓ My job does not have enough variety.

Pay satisfaction

✓ I believe I am fairly paid compared to my peers at *<insert name of organization>* who are at equivalent job levels and who are equally skilled.

✓ I believe I am fairly paid compared to my peers in other organizations who are at equivalent job levels and who are equally skilled.

✓ I am satisfied with my total compensation.

Supervisor support

✓ My supervisor is willing to help me when I need a special favor.

✓ My supervisor would forgive an honest mistake on my part.

✓ My supervisor really cares about my well-being.

✓ My supervisor fails to appreciate any extra effort from me (*reverse coded*).

Thriving—Vitality

✓ I feel energetic and vital at work.

✓ I do not feel very energetic at work (*reversed*).

✓ I feel alert and awake at work.

✓ I look forward to each new day at work.

Thriving—Learning

✓ I find myself learning often.

✓ I continue to learn more as time goes by.

✓ I see myself continually improving.

✓ I am not learning (*reversed*).

✓ I am developing a lot as a person.

Work-life balance

✓ The demands of my work interfere with my home and personal/family life.

✓ The amount of time my job takes up

makes it difficult to fulfill personal/
family duties.

- ✓ My job produces strain that makes
  it difficult to fulfill personal/family
  obligations.
- ✓ Due to work-related duties, I have
  to make changes to my plans for
  personal/family activities.

Group/unit/organization-focused constructs

Commitment to organization <*insert name of
organization*>

- ✓ I do not feel like "part of the family" at
  _____ (*reversed*).
- ✓ I do not feel "emotionally attached" to
  _____ (*reversed*).
- ✓ _____ has a great deal of personal
  meaning for me.
- ✓ I feel a strong sense of belonging to
  _____.

Commitment to team

- ✓ I do not feel like "part of the family"
  on my team (*reversed*).
- ✓ I do not feel "emotionally attached" to
  my team (*reversed*).
- ✓ My team has a great deal of personal
  meaning for me.

✓ I feel a strong sense of belonging to my team.

IT support

✓ We waste considerable time in doing our work because of information technology problems that are not fixed (*reversed*).

✓ Our organization provides adequate information technology support.

✓ We receive prompt technical assistance when our computer systems are not working.

Organizational support *<insert name of organization>*

✓ _____ is willing to help me when I need a special favor.

✓ _____ would forgive an honest mistake on my part.

✓ _____ really cares about my well-being.

✓ _____ fails to appreciate any extra effort from me (*reverse coded*).

Rewards for team performance

✓ My pay depends on the success of the teams I work with.

✓ Pay is tied to team performance.

✓ My contributions to this team are rewarded by *<insert name of organization>*.

Shared understanding

✓ People on my team do not agree on what is really important (*reversed*).

✓ We have a shared understanding of what we are trying to accomplish on my team.

✓ There is agreement about our priorities on my team.

✓ There is an agreed way of getting the work done on my team.

Trust in team members

✓ Team members always do what they say they will do.

✓ The people on my team are reliable in their work.

✓ Team members believe that others on our team will follow through on their commitments.

REFERENCES

Albrecht, Simon, ed. (2010). *Handbook of Employee Engagement.* Cheltenham, England: Edward Elgar Publishing Limited.

Anderson, Donald L. (2011). *Organization Development: The Process of Leading Organizational Change.* Thousand Oaks, CA: Sage Publications.

Bakker, Arnold, and Michael Leiter, eds. (2010). *Work Engagement: A Handbook of Essential Theory and Research.* New York: Psychology Press.

Bradburn, Norman, Seymour Sudman, and Brian Wansink (2004). *Asking Questions: The Definitive Guide to Questionnaire Design—For Market Research, Political Polls, and Social and Health Questionnaires.* San Francisco: Jossey-Bass.

Cheung-Judge, Mee-Yan, and Linda Holbeche (2012). *Organization Development: A Practitioner's Guide for OD and HR.* Philadelphia: Kogan Page Limited.

Church, Allan, and Janine Waclawski, eds. (2001). *Designing and Using Organizational Surveys: A Seven-step Process.* San Francisco: Jossey-Bass.

Cummings, Thomas G., and Christopher G. Worley (2008). *Organization Development and Change.* Mason, OH: Cengage Learning.

DeVellis, Robert F. (2012). *Scale Development: Theory and Applications*, Third Edition. Applied Social Research Methods Series 26. Thousand Oaks, CA: Sage Publications.

Fields, Dail L. (2002). *Taking the Measure of Work: A Guide to Validated Scales for Organizational Research and Diagnosis.* Thousand Oaks, CA: Sage Publications.

Fink, Arlene (2013). *How to Conduct Surveys: A Step-by-Step Guide.* Thousand Oaks, CA: Sage Publications.

Fowler, Floyd Jr. (2009). *Survey Research Methods*, Applied Social Research Methods Series 1, Thousand Oaks, CA: Sage Publications.

Gallos, Joan V. (2006). *Organization Development: A Jossey-Bass Reader.* San Francisco: Jossey-Bass.

Harter, James K., Frank L. Schmidt, and Theodore L. Hayes (2002). "Business-unit-level relationship between employee satisfaction, employee engagement, and business outcomes: A meta-analysis". *Journal of Applied Psychology*, 87:2, 268–279.

Heskett, James L., W. Earl Sasser, and Leonard A. Schlesinger (1997). *The Service Profit Chain*. New York: The Free Press.

Kador, John, and Katherine Armstrong (2010). *Perfect Phrases for Writing Employee Surveys: Hundreds of Ready-to-Use Phrases to Help You Create Surveys Your Employees Answer Honestly, Completely, and Helpfully*. New York: McGraw-Hill.

Kraut, Allen, ed. (1996). *Organizational Surveys: Tools for Assessment and Change*. San Francisco: Jossey-Bass.

Kraut, Allen, ed. (2006). *Getting Action from Organizational Surveys*. San Francisco: Jossey-Bass.

Levenson, Alec, and Tracy Faber (2009). "Using human capital measurement to drive productivity". *HR Magazine*, 68–74, June.

Levenson, Alec, Michael J. Fenlon, and George Benson (2010). "Rethinking retention strategies: Work-life versus deferred compensation in a total rewards strategy". *WorldatWork Journal*, November.

Levenson, Alec, Wim Van der Stede, and Susan Cohen (2006). "Measuring the relationship between managerial competencies and performance". *Journal of Management*, 32(3), 360–380.

Macey, William, Benjamin Schneider, Karen Barbera, and Scott Young (2009). *Employee Engagement: Tools for Analysis, Practice, and Competitive Advantage.* Chichester, West Sussex: John Wiley & Sons.

McConnell, John (2003). *How to Design, Implement, and Interpret an Employee Survey.* New York: AMACOM.

Rucci, Anthony J., Steven P. Kirn, and Richard T. Quinn (1998). "The Employee-Customer-Profit Chain at Sears". *Harvard Business Review*, Vol. 76, No. 1, January.

INDEX

Note: an *f* indicates a figure; a *t*, a table.

ACKNOWLEDGMENTS

This book reflects the collective wisdom of decades of research, practice, and partnering with companies at the Center for Effective Organizations (CEO) in the Marshall School of Business at University of Southern California.

Over the past fifteen years that I have worked at CEO, I have learned from some of the best in the business how to apply survey tools and action research methodologies to investigate issues of importance related to people and organizational processes. The colleagues who have trained, mentored, and collaborated with me include George Benson, John Boudreau, Jay Conger, Jennifer Deal, David

Finegold, Mike Gibbs, Cris Gibson, Ed Lawler, Sue Mohrman, Jim O'Toole, Maritza Salazar, Sarah Stawiski, Mark Van Buren, Wim Van der Stede, Theresa Welbourne, Wenhong (Sarah) Zhang, and Cindy Zoghi. I owe a special debt of gratitude to our dearly departed colleague, Susan Cohen, my first mentor at CEO and a true friend whose contributions to the field were cut short way too early in her career. We miss you, Susan.

The work we do at CEO is expertly supported by our outstanding research staff, both past and present, including Nora Osganian, Alice Mark, Aaron Griffith, Beth Neilson, and Jessica Schoner. Without them, none of the work that serves as the foundation of this book would ever have happened.

I owe a debt of gratitude to the countless professionals and practitioners who have collaborated with and contributed to the work I have done in organizations. Especially important have been the partnerships with Allison Baker, Jeff Bennett, Joe Bonito, Jane Dobie, Anne Donovan, Mike Fenlon, Anne Fithern, Eric Ingram, Nancy Jagmin, Bianca Martorella, Patrick McLaughlin, Mike McDermott, Ben Nemo, Per Scott, Scott Stevenson, Kim Warmbier, Tracy Witt, and Inge Zhang.

Special thanks go to the editors, reviewers, and staff at Berrett-Koehler and the Society for Human Resource Management, especially Steve Piersanti and Chris Anzalone. The idea for this book started as a short article and evolved into a much more thorough treatment of the issues because of their encouragement, advice, and assistance.

ABOUT THE AUTHOR

Dr. Levenson is Senior Research Scientist at the Center for Effective Organizations in the Marshall School of Business, University of Southern California. His action research and consulting with companies optimizes job and organization performance and HR systems through the application of organization design, job design, and human capital analytics.

Alec's work with companies combines the best elements of scientific research and practical, actionable knowledge that companies can use to improve performance. He draws from the disciplines of economics, strategy, organization behavior, and industrial-organizational psychology to tackle complex talent and organizational challenges that defy easy solutions. His recommendations focus on the actions organizations should take to make lasting improvements in critical structures and processes.

Alec has spent over a decade training human resource professionals and teams in the application of human capital analytics, from a broad range of Fortune 500 and Global 500 companies. The tools and models are adapted from the scientific literature and applied to diagnose every aspect of data from surveys to interviews/focus groups, performance ratings, operational metrics, HRIS systems, and more.

His research has been published in numerous academic and business publications and featured in major media outlets including *New York Times, Wall Street Journal, The Economist, CNN, Associated Press, U.S. News and World Report, National Public Radio, USA Today, Marketplace,* and *Fox News*. He received his PhD and MA in Economics from Princeton University and his BA in Economics and Chinese language (double major) from University of Wisconsin-Madison.

SOCIETY FOR HUMAN
RESOURCE MANAGEMENT

Founded in 1948, the Society for Human Resource Management (SHRM) is the world's largest HR membership organization devoted to human resource management. Representing more than 275,000 members in over 160 countries, the Society is the leading provider of resources to serve the needs of HR professionals and advance the professional practice of human resource management. SHRM has more than 575 affiliated chapters within the United States and subsidiary offices in China, India, and United Arab Emirates. Visit us at shrm.org.

Berrett–Koehler
Publishers

Berrett-Koehler is an independent publisher dedicated to an ambitious mission: *Creating a World That Works for All*.

We believe that to truly create a better world, action is needed at all levels—individual, organizational, and societal. At the individual level, our publications help people align their lives with their values and with their aspirations for a better world. At the organizational level, our publications promote progressive leadership and management practices, socially responsible approaches to business, and humane and effective organizations. At the societal level, our publications advance social and economic justice, shared prosperity, sustainability, and new solutions to national and global issues.

A major theme of our publications is "Opening Up New Space." Berrett-Koehler titles challenge conventional thinking, introduce new ideas, and foster positive change. Their common quest is changing the underlying beliefs, mindsets, institutions, and structures that keep generating the same cycles of problems, no matter who our leaders are or what improvement programs we adopt.

We strive to practice what we preach—to operate our publishing company in line with the ideas in our books. At the core of our approach is stewardship, which we define as a deep sense of responsibility to administer the company for the benefit of all of our "stakeholder" groups: authors, customers, employees, investors, service providers, and the communities and environment around us.

We are grateful to the thousands of readers, authors, and other friends of the company who consider themselves to be part of the "BK Community." We hope that you, too, will join us in our mission.

A BK Business Book

This book is part of our BK Business series. BK Business titles pioneer new and progressive leadership and management practices in all types of public, private, and nonprofit organizations. They promote socially responsible approaches to business, innovative organizational change methods, and more humane and effective organizations.

Berrett–Koehler
Publishers

A community dedicated to creating
a world that works for all

Dear Reader,

Thank you for picking up this book and joining our worldwide community of Berrett-Koehler readers. We share ideas that bring positive change into people's lives, organizations, and society.

To welcome you, we'd like to offer you a free e-book. You can pick from among twelve of our bestselling books by entering the promotional code BKP92E here: http://www.bkconnection.com/welcome.

When you claim your free e-book, we'll also send you a copy of our e-newsletter, the *BK Communiqué*. Although you're free to unsubscribe, there are many benefits to sticking around. In every issue of our newsletter you'll find

- A free e-book
- Tips from famous authors
- Discounts on spotlight titles
- Hilarious insider publishing news
- A chance to win a prize for answering a riddle

Best of all, our readers tell us, "Your newsletter is the only one I actually read." So claim your gift today, and please stay in touch!

Sincerely,

Charlotte Ashlock
Steward of the BK Website

Questions? Comments? Contact me at bkcommunity@bkpub.com.

MIX
From responsible sources
FSC® C113845
www.fsc.org

Certified

Corporation
bcorporation.net